EXPANDING
OUR NOW

Also by Harrison Owen

Spirit: Transformation and Development in Organizations

Leadership Is

Riding the Tiger

The Millennium Organization

Tales From Open Space

Open Space Technology: A User's Guide

EXPANDING OUR NOW

The Story of
Open Space Technology

HARRISON OWEN

Berrett-Koehler Publishers, Inc.
San Francisco

The author is grateful to Threshold Books, 139 Main St., Brattleboro, VT 05301 for permission to reprint the lines from *Open Secret: Versions of Rumi* as they appear on page 134.

Berrett–Koehler Publishers, Inc.
450 Sansome Street, Suite 1200
San Francisco, CA 94611-3320
Tel: (415) 288-0260   Fax: (415) 362-2512

ORDERING INFORMATION

Individual sales. Berrett-Koehler publications are available through most bookstores. They can also be ordered direct from Berrett-Koehler at the address above.

Quantity sales. Special discounts are available on quantity purchases by corporations, associations, and others. For details, contact the "Special Sales Department" at the Berrett-Koehler address above.

Orders for college textbook/course adoption use.
Please contact Berrett-Koehler Publishers at the address above.

Orders by U.S. trade bookstores and wholesalers.
Please contact Publishers Group West, 4065 Hollis Street, Box 8843, Emeryville, CA 94662. Tel: (510) 658-3453; 1-800-788-3123. Fax: (510) 658-1834

Printed in the United States of America

Printed on acid-free and recycled paper that is composed of 85% recovered fiber, including 15% post consumer waste).

Library of Congress Cataloging–in–Publication Data

Owen, Harrison, 1935–
Expanding our now : the story of open space technology / Harrison Owen.
          p.   cm.

     Includes bibliographical references and index.
     ISBN 1-57675-015-9 (alk. paper)
1. Decision-making, Group. 2. Spatial behavior, I. Title.
     HD30.23.O925   1997
     658.4'036––dc21

                                                            97-17806
                                                            CIP

First Edition
  00 99 98 97   10 9 8 7 6 5 4 3 2 1

Cover and text designed by Greene Design
Cover photography by Brad Greene

Table of Contents

Prologue

*O*pen Space Technology is, at the very least, a new way to hold better meetings. The normative experience is that groups, large and small (from five to one thousand members), self-organize to effectively deal with hugely complex issues in a very short time. Overt facilitation is minimal to nonexistent, and preplanning, so far as the agenda is concerned, never happens.

In a word, Open Space is fast, economical, and effective, but it is more than a mega–monster–meeting–manager. For me, it is a metaphor for life and a means to navigate our curious environment as we approach the millennium. In effect, Open Space has become a natural laboratory in which to perceive and explore the emerging potential of our common humanity in a transforming world. The starting point may be better meetings, but the endpoint is richer ways of being together in that wonderful thing we call *organization*.

The emerging interest in Whole Systems Interventions (sometimes referred to as Large Systems Interventions) has recently provided a useful context for the discussion of Open Space. The genesis of this interest is a growing realization that efforts toward organizational change, when addressed at the level of the individual or even small groups, move too slowly to keep pace with today's challenges. By the time all members of an organization have been run through whatever change process is being utilized, the world has changed once again. We have been dealt that wonderful card telling us, "Return to Start."

A useful alternative appears to be to get the whole system in one room at the same time, thereby accomplishing in a short period what might ordinarily take years. In order to do this, approaches other than traditional are essential, in large part because traditional approaches were designed for individuals and small groups. In response to today's need, a number of new methods have appeared, such as Future Search, Real Time Strategic Change, Simu–Real, and of course, Open Space Technology.

Billye Alban and Barbara Bunker have chronicled this phenomenon in *Large Group Interventions: Engaging the Whole System for Rapid Change* (Jossey–Bass, 1997). Each of the new approaches has similarities and differences, and no one approach is useful or effective in all situations. I leave the essential "compare and contrast" in the capable hands of these authors, reserving for myself the only task I feel competent to perform: telling the story of Open Space as I have experienced it.

My name is closely associated with Open Space, which might lead people to assume that I designed it with infinite patience and great care. This would be an error. As I see it, Open Space has always existed, or it has recently emerged by itself. My privilege has been simply to stumble upon it.

This discovery has not been a solo act. Indeed, there are literally thousands of people around the world who, over a period of a dozen years, have made substantive contributions to the discovery of Open Space either as practitioners, participants, or just onlookers. This book is a testimony to them, for in truth the discovery has been, and remains, a collaborative one.

What follows is essentially a personal account of that collaborative journey. It may therefore be useful to offer a brief autobiography, indicating some of the paths and byways that subsequently have become formative to my understanding of Open Space, as well as my understanding of everything else.

Forty years ago, my path was clear. I was going to be a priest (Anglican/Episcopalian). Not a parish priest but an academic. My passion, through almost ten years of seminary and graduate school, was the function of mythology in the culture of the ancient Near East, combined with a continuing interest in chaos and order as constituent elements of the creative process. Season the mix well with a heavy dose of epistemology, the study of how we know, and you have the makings of an esoteric academic career.

That career was trashed with the bombing of two Black churches in Birmingham, Alabama. Suddenly, library stacks were replaced with city streets, where I found myself organizing and demonstrating. This new life work became a job when I moved to Washington, D.C., and became the executive director of the Adams–Morgan Community Council, a large multiracial neighborhood association.

Two years later, I was off to the West Coast of Africa. As a Peace Corps associate director, I was responsible for 150 volunteers in Monrovia, the capital city of Liberia.

Two more years and I was back in the United States to direct a health–care infrastructure–building program on Long Island. Then came a stint at the National Institutes of Health, developing and directing the patient, public, and professional education programs for the National Heart, Lung and Blood Institute. My last honest job was at the Veterans Administration as a political appointee in the Carter administration. I held the curious title of Confidential Special Assistant to the Chief Medical Director, with special responsibility for the Senior Executive Development Programs and the National Advisory Council.

When it became clear that Jimmy Carter was not to be reelected president, I moved in yet another direction and established H. H. Owen and Company, which has been my venue for operating since 1979. From the start it was a huge enterprise, consisting of me in all roles–with able assistance from my wife, Ethelyn, and (under duress) my children.

H. H. Owen and Co. has been a little open space in which to focus the apparently disparate elements of my life. I found that my seemingly esoteric interests–mythology, culture, chaos, order, and creation, to say nothing of epistemology–had all provided subtle guidance as I wandered along African trails and through the halls of government, and subsequently these interests have provided the basis of my work with a broad range of clients all over the world, from Fortune 500 companies to small third–world villages. And of course, along the way came Open Space Technology. The intent of this book is to record the salient details of my experience with Open Space and to offer such interpretations as I feel comfortable with.

Open Space is somewhat problematical because it flies in the face of many currently accepted practices and principles of meeting and organizational management. Indeed, according to accepted practice, Open Space should not work at all. But since it does work, perhaps it is we who do not need to toil quite so hard at preparation for meetings and at other organizational tasks. To borrow the title from the recent book by Margaret Wheatley and Myron Kellner–Rogers, Open Space may be described as "a simpler way."

One day over lunch, a senior official from the American Society for Training and Development (ASTD) remarked that if what I had just told him about Open Space was true (and he insisted that he wasn't questioning my veracity), then "95 percent of what we are currently doing does not need to be done." A young associate added her feeling that the number was actually closer to 99 percent.

On the question of what works with Open Space, I can only tell the story as I have experienced it, while simultaneously inviting you, the reader, to try it for yourself and draw your own conclusions.

On the related question of why and how Open Space works, I offer my best guesses—backed up by a lifetime's work in and about organizations of all sorts—but still guesses for all of that. Someday it will be possible to write the definitive book with the appropriate footnotes, but that day has not arrived, nor is this that book.

Carrying my disclaimer one step further, please be aware that this present offering is not a "how-to" book. The practical details of working in Open Space will be found in *Open Space Technology: A User's Guide* (second edition, Berrett-Koehler, 1997).

At this juncture, you may be wondering why you should bother reading this book. After all, it is admittedly filled with stories and guesses, not the essential "how-to-do-it" information. The answer, I think, is all about Now.

Now is a funny thing. It is all we have, and yet there seems to be nothing there. Ask anyone about the duration of Now, and it can be this week, this day, this hour, this minute—then *poof*—it virtually disappears. By definition, neither the past nor the future exist: the past is over and the future hasn't happened yet. All we have is Now, and it seems always to be slipping through our fingers.

When Now disappears or shrinks to an instant, life is swallowed up by regret for the past and anxiety for the future. The window of opportunity—Now—is painfully small.

Were it possible to expand our Now, at the very least there would be more time/space for doing what needs to get done. Stress and strain levels might actually decline as it would no longer be necessary to race, at breakneck speed, away from an omnivorous past and headlong into a threatening future. We could just enjoy Now.

I believe the ultimate gift of Open Space is the expansion of our Now. If that idea appeals to you, you have sufficient reason to continue reading this story.

Chapter I

East Meets West

*I*t was not the first time Open Space Technology was used, but it was significant nonetheless. Executives from the Taj Group of Hotels, part of the Tata family of businesses in India, had resonated positively to my 1988 paper, *The Business of Business Is Learning*, and decided that a conference on the subject would be beneficial. In support of that undertaking, they offered their exquisite conference center at Fort Aguada, Goa—with all expenses paid. Why we used Open Space is somewhat of a mystery, but it seemed like a good idea at the time. Subsequent experience suggests that it was probably an idea whose time had come.

Support also came from Procter and Gamble, giving birth to a second, parallel conference in Berkeley Springs, West Virginia. It, too, was conducted in Open Space and broadly expanded our emerging understanding of learning in organizations. However, since the intent of the moment is to introduce Open Space, I will leave the details of that conference for another time.

Goa is an interesting place. Located on the subcontinent of India, this tropical paradise is an ancient mix of East and West. Once a Portuguese colony, Goa officially (and forcibly) rejoined the life of the East after India's declaration of independence. There is a definite Western presence here, but it exists within the deep consciousness of Mother India.

In response to the kind invitation of the Taj Group, Indian executives, theoreticians, academics, and consultants joined their colleagues from the United States, the United Kingdom, and Europe. We had the president of a computer company, senior executives from the Indian steel industry, and two professors of management, one from London and the other from Bombay. There was even a television producer from Seattle. Fifty souls in all, they were drawn together by a common fascination with learning in organizations, and an even deeper conviction that life at the end of the twentieth, soon to be the twenty-first, century demanded incessant learning if organizations were going to survive, and hopefully prosper.

Since that time, the notion of the learning organization has become almost banal. But in those days, the concept of learning in organizations, and more especially of organizations that learn, was a new idea. To be sure, training departments abounded in all the "best" organizations, but real, deep learning of the sort that bursts paradigms and charts new courses for humanity was simply not to be found in the day-to-day life of businesses, governments, and related social institutions. Better to leave learning to the halls of academe, and never confuse it with the ongoing task of making a living.

So it was for many years. But the conflicting, not to mention catastrophic forces sweeping the planet made one thing very clear: what we took for granted yesterday is suspect today and quite likely will be "off the screen" by the end of the week. Ongoing learning, imagining and creating realities that never were, expanding our awareness of the nature of our world, all have become issues of first concern. The alternatives are not acceptable. And so we gathered in Goa.

It Was Bizarre

If the topic was esoteric, the mode of meeting was downright bizarre. In spite of the academic and executive fixation on advance agenda preparation, there was none. In fact, all we had was a theme, a starting time, and a concluding time. All the rest was open space— to be filled with whatever meaning and intent we, the participants, might desire.

We began in a circle, all fifty of us sitting on small conference room chairs, gazing anxiously and expectantly at our colleagues, face to face. It was a pretty big circle, and it appeared even bigger than its actual physical dimensions because most of us did not know each other, except for brief biographical details that were hardly comforting. The word diverse was appropriate but did small justice to the reality. We were, quite literally, from different worlds. Held in common was a belief that doing business as we had always done business was a certain prescription for going out of business. I suppose we also shared an appreciation of high adventure, going where others had never quite gone before.

In the center of the circle were a small stack of paper, some marking pens, and a few packages of blu–tac, the European/Indian equivalent of masking tape. There was also a large, shallow beaten–copper dish, perhaps a meter across, filled with water and covered with floating flower petals arranged in a meticulously beautiful design. As we considered each other and the three days lying ahead, the openness of the circle created by our presence appeared almost as a cosmic void, a great emptiness, the battleground for mythic drama, the home of chaos. A little far out perhaps, but quite reflective of the fleeting thoughts passing through most of our minds. How on earth did we ever permit ourselves to show up under such questionable circumstances, sitting with fifty strangers, no agenda, and three days to fill?

But it was the flowers that caught our eyes and interpreted the moment. Each person, no matter where they sat, found the view filtered and informed by the exquisite loveliness of those floating petals. In the midst of chaos, there was a center point of beauty and order. Clearly, Toto, this was not Kansas.

As a convener of the group, I rose to welcome the participants. Walking slowly around the inside of the circle, I invited each of our guests to spend a moment, before the festivities began, allowing their eyes to trace the circle of their peers, acknowledging the few that they knew, and making initial contact with the strangers. By the time I had completed my circumnavigation, a surprising and unexpressed intimacy manifested in the open space, and then it was on to the business. Briskly moving to the center of the circle, I described our theme: *The Business of Business Is Learning*, which of course was also the title of my paper. Each person who cared to do so was invited to identify any area or issue related to our theme for which they had some genuine passion and were prepared to take personal responsibility, as in convening a session around their concern. With their issue in mind, they were to come to the center of the circle, take one of the pieces of paper, and with a marking pen, inscribe their theme on the paper, sign their name, announce their name and theme to the group, and post their paper on the wall. They were to indicate a time and a place to meet, which could be their room, by the pool, or even on the beach.

While each individual contemplated their response (or sat in still somewhat shocked silence), I proposed four principles and one law to guide our interactions with one another.

The Four Principles

1. *Whoever comes is the right people,* which reminds us that it is not how many people show up, their title or position, but rather the fact that they share, in some way, our passion, which makes all the difference, and therefore qualifies them as the "right" people.
2. *Whatever happens is the only thing that could have,* which directs our attention away from what might have been, could have been, or should have been, and anchors our regard firmly in what is— right now.
3. *Whenever it starts is the right time,* which suggests that when it comes to creative interchange and spirited inquiry, the clock is not the final arbiter. Things start when they are ready—not before and not later.
4. *When it's over, it's over,* which means just what it says. Don't waste time when the moment has passed. Move on to something useful.

The One Law

The Law of Two Feet, which might also be called the law of mobility for those who are differently abled, is pretty much what you might suspect. If at any time during the time together, anyone finds that they are neither contributing nor learning, they should use their two feet and move. Individuals alone are responsible for the quality of their experience and the giving of their gifts.

With the principles outlined and the law announced, the action could begin. Each person was invited to come forward with that which had heart and meaning for them, write it down, announce it to the group, and post it on the wall. And off we went.

To the surprise of everybody, we did just that. Normal reserve evaporated as a dozen people lay down on the floor by the flower petals, scribbling furiously, and then stood up to gain the attention of the group. When the first group finished, more came, and so it went until the wall was covered with more than enough to keep us involved and busy, not only for the three days immediately at hand, but as it has turned out, for many years to come. When at last no more items were offered, the entire group approached the wall en masse to sign up for the discussion groups that everyone wished to attend.

And what went up on the wall? An amazing array of stuff. From Prasad Kaipa, at that point dean of Apple University, we got, "What Is Learning?" Another contribution was, "Learning as Transformation," and so it went. Scarcely an hour had passed since our start, and we were into the thick of things. Groups were forming in their desig-nated places, discussions of great intensity were breaking out all over. Somehow, someway, the great void of the open space that separated us had been crossed.

The day passed with group following group, lapping and overlap-ping each other. Discussions begun in one place continued on the way to another, and by evening when we assembled for what we called Evening News, it was one tired but very alive assemblage of people. Apparently without trying, and almost invisibly, the bonds of community formed. Strangers became acquaintances and then fellow travelers on a marvelous journey of exploration.

On the morning of the second day, we met briefly to adjust our agenda, adding items that had popped up in the discussions and tak-ing some items down when the proposers felt the areas had already been covered.

The Impact of Honesty

But just as we were about to depart for another full day of discussions, one of our number spoke up. Very directly and with great feeling, Prasad Kaipa said what in any other circumstance would have been unsayable, and indeed unthinkable. "I have learned nothing! It is true that we have had great conversation, and the erudition is immense, but it is conversation I have heard before. I've been there and done that, and I don't need to do it again. Unless we can get beyond where we have all been, the journey will have been wasted."

Silence. But not shocked silence. We all agreed. There had indeed been great conversation, but most, if not all, had dealt with the known, the experienced, what the "literature" said. There had been a great deal of "head" talk, but somehow the heart was missing. In a word, we had been playing it safe.

Had this been any other conference, the silence *would* have been shocked, followed by a hasty call to the planning committee for an instant session of blame fixing and conference redesign. But we were the planning committee, and it was quite clear where the responsibility lay. Following a brief discussion, it was apparent to all that the fault lay not with the topics on the wall, but rather with our collective willingness to dig deeply. And after all, there is not much point in talking about that sort of stuff. You just do it. And so we did.

It is a little hard to describe what happened next. It had much more to do with the quality of feelings and the intensity of conversation than any obvious substantive output, although there was substantive output in abundance. The focus continued on issues such as, "What Is Learning?" combined with the elaboration of concrete approaches to the creation of organizational environments in which genuine learning could take place. But it was all somehow deeper, richer, riskier, and definitely "out there."

Breaking Through

Something of the flavor may be savored in an emergent theme that, curiously enough, crossed several groups and quite literally swirled about the total environment. *Learning is the evolution of consciousness, and the function of organizations is to create the environment in which such evolution might take place.*

The phrase "evolution of human consciousness" is not found in the majority of business texts, and the suggestion that organizations, specifically businesses, should have any obligation to foster such a thing may appear to some as odd. But that is precisely what fifty consultants, management professors, and senior executives found themselves immersed in. Beneath the practical details of everyday organizational experience, there exists a deeper reality—the human Spirit—what some might call consciousness. That Spirit gives life to the organization; therefore, the growth of the organization requires the growth of Spirit, or the evolution of consciousness, which might be considered the essence of learning. At least that was the idea.

Where it all began is hard to say, and a truthful answer might well be: everywhere and nowhere. Fertile soil was doubtless provided by the hugely divergent experiences and cultures of the participants, an astonishing blend of East and West. But East and West have met before, and more often than not, the result has been assimilation of one to the other. Western rationalism and practicality dominate the Eastern depths, or the reverse occurs and the West disappears in a miasma of Eastern nothingness. But something new was manifest:

neither one nor the other, and also not the lowest common denomi-
nator of the two.

One conversation sticks in my mind as a representative point of
genesis. A very senior Indian executive, Jagdish Parikh, started to play
with the notion of a *business yoga*, somehow uniting the ancient spiritual practices that lie at the core of the Indian experience with the
hard practicalities of his business world. Location of the precise point
of genesis, in fact, makes little difference, for what began as a wisp of
an idea quickly assumed the power of a rolling wave, passing through
groups and uniting all in a common flow of energy.

The effect was contagious; for as the sense of flow intensified, two
apparently opposite entities, the individual and the collective, gathered strength, focus, and direction.

Those of us who reside in the West generally hold that the individual is supreme, and as power rises with the collective, the individual is at risk. Stereotypically, the East holds exactly the opposite point
of view: maximize the individual and the collective is at risk. The
experience in Goa would confirm neither.

As a Westerner, I found my awareness of the collective's power becoming a matter of almost morbid fascination. I was enthralled with
the incredible sense of unity with folks known to me for only a very
short period of time, and positively terrified that my uniqueness would
be swallowed whole. But each time I was sure my individuality would
be sacrificed it reemerged again—whole, new, and more powerful.
Truly a learning experience. One might even say transformational.

Results?

Three and one-half days from the start, our conference was over. It
would be reasonable to ask what had happened, and what did it all

mean anyhow? An immediate answer would be that each one of us was profoundly aware that something of significance had occurred. We had done what we all knew, or suspected, at the start to be impossible. Fifty powerful individuals from multiple cultures and places had self-organized a three-day gathering concerned with hugely complex and emotion-laden issues. There had been no prior agenda-setting, no planning committee, no cadre of facilitators, no angry walkouts. Conflict, discomfort, and confrontation, although certainly present, had always led to deeper insights and understandings. In a word, it had felt good. Better than good, it had been fun in the deepest sense. There had been a reverent playfulness that honored the unique contribution of every participant, respecting the differences and somehow driving to the depths (heights?) of an extraordinary human experience full of learning and joy.

I suppose that sort of experience, in and of itself, might be sufficient justification for the event, but there was more. And with each passing year, the dimensions of that "more" seem only to expand. One of the curious aftershocks of the gathering has been the fact that the vast majority (indeed, maybe even the totality) of the participants are now doing something significantly different from what they were doing at the time. The shifts range from totally new life works to interior shifts of personal vision and self-understanding, which have vested everyday activities with radically different motivation and rationale.

It is an interesting chicken and egg question. Did the participants self-select because they were on the verge of fundamental transition, or did the gathering itself initiate these transitions? The question is unanswerable, but it is also probably moot in as much as the consensus appears to be that whether causative or coincidental, the shifts took place close on the heels of the event. Indeed, some even had a clear view of where the shift would lead them prior to our departure from Goa.

On a more substantive level, the discussions begun at Goa have been generative of a veritable tidal wave of literary production. Frankly, I have rather lost count, but my best recollection is that something like fifteen books subsequently emerged from the experience.

The conference itself has now become a regular repeat performance in India. The specific theme shifts from year to year, but many of the fundamentals remain, particularly around the understanding of learning at deeper levels. Never far from the surface is also an interest in what might now be called *Indian management*. We have all heard about Japanese management, American management, and European management, but the unique contributions of India are now coming into view. As some of us from the West put it in the course of our discussions, "What are the special insights regarding the human condition and organizational performance that may be gleaned from five thousand years of Indian tradition?" Clearly a lot of folks have been thinking a lot of things for a long time. What can we all learn from that?

And Prasad? What happened to Prasad Kaipa? Upon returning to the United States, he left his position at Apple Computer to engage full-time in a pursuit of a deeper understanding of learning. He consults with a broad range of American and Indian corporations, and even uses Open Space in his practice. Best of all, he remains a close colleague and friend of mine.

In terms of our present story, the Goa experience was a clear start point in the use of Open Space globally. What had begun as a novel and untried approach to conference planning has assumed, much to my surprise, a powerful presence in the unending search for better ways to enhance the quality and productivity of the human endeavor. Obviously there was much to learn, and in fact we have been learning much ever since. There was, however, a new kid on the block.

All About Now

But who is that kid? What is the story? With the wisdom of hindsight, and no little subsequent reflection, it seems to me that it is all about Now, and more specifically, about expanding Now.

Just think about it: all we really have is Now. We acknowledge that the past is over and the future hasn't happened yet. We live Now. It is really quite simple. But how long is Now? This year? This month? Today? This instant? Looked at one way, Now vanishes into a nano-second. Look again, and everything is Now, for neither the past nor the future truly exist, or so we say. It almost seems like we have a choice in the matter, and Now can be any size we want.

But why would anybody care? At one level, I suppose, contemplating the extent of Now is rather like asking how many angels dance on the head of a pin: interesting thought but scarcely of great utility. Still, every single one of us plants our feet firmly in the here and now. Furthermore, we never seem to have enough Now. What would be different about having a big Now? Or a little one? A lot, I think.

As a matter of fact, I believe most folks have tiny little Nows. They live in this instant only, and this instant is a very small one. The past is racing forward to gobble it up, and the future intrudes to hem it in. And when your Now is very small, everything with any kind of meaning is quickly pushed into the past, where it can be reached only by memory, usually with regret. Or it resides in the future, accessible only through hope accompanied by anxiety. We are left with precious little, save our anxious memories and fearful expectations. Not a happy place to be.

Individuals are not the only creatures with restricted Nows. Corporations and social institutions seem to suffer from a similar malady. It is called concentration on short–term results and fixation on the next quarter's numbers. Other signs of a tiny Now are inability to see the big picture and myopia in terms of new opportunities that may lie just outside what we are currently doing.

Perhaps the most unnerving symptom of a restricted Now is the anxiety–provoking rat race of trying to fit everything in. After all, when we live within a tiny Now, the events of our lives race by the narrow slit of our vision at a mind–numbing pace—out of the future and into the past in the blink of an eye. It's enough to stress out anyone.

What we need is a bigger Now. When we have a broader vista and a wider perspective, the race of events from the future to the past slows to a manageable rate. The window of opportunity expands considerably.

Expanding our Now is what Open Space is all about. At least that was the learning of Goa, which has been constantly confirmed in the succeeding years. We began by sitting in a circle confronting strangers, separated by a vast (or so it seemed) stretch of nothingness, which was mirrored by the equivalent blankness of our agenda. There was a theme, and supposedly we knew why we were there, and maybe we knew a little bit about where we might be going. But none of us, absolutely none of us, had even the smallest appreciation for the distance we would travel or the magnitude of the realities we would collectively bring into the arena of our awareness.

The experience of Open Space in Goa was the experience of a constantly expanding circle, of including more and more in our consciousness—more people, more cultures, more traditions. Stimulating gifts from five thousand years of human enterprise filled our Now to overflowing. Many, perhaps most of us, started with a very limited view of what learning was all about, derived from our experience at school or in the corporate training department. We even thought we knew what we were doing and what ought to be done. Were we ever wrong! We didn't know the half of it. But things changed in a hurry, and definitely for the better. That is the story of Goa, and it appears to be the continuing story of Open Space.

Not all of the Open Space happenings are as esoteric or exotic as Goa, but they do manifest common features. Diverse people facing complex issues, for whom conflict is a present reality or a real possibility, nevertheless manage to achieve quite uncommon results—quickly and with a sense of pride. As a bonus, there is usually a profound sense of playfulness and joy. Best of all, Now expands, and then continues to expand.

The expanding Now, the story of Open Space, is what I propose to explore in the following pages—not exhaustively, but hopefully with sufficient detail to intrigue you into further exploration on your own. We will consider how Open Space evolved (chapter 2) and the experience to date (chapter 3). Then it will be on to the more interesting (to me) questions of why it works (chapters 4 through 6) and where we might be headed next (chapter 7). The final chapter attempts to pull all the pieces together, more or less.

I make no pretense to have all the answers, but I do intend to share my experience, recognizing that others may, and indeed do, have a different experience. If this book works, you will be persuaded to develop your own experience.

Chapter II

Open Space Discovered

*O*pen Space Technology came into being by way of a joke made
out of frustration. The frustration was mine, when at the conclusion of a year–long effort to organize an international symposium
for 250 souls, everybody agreed the best part had been the coffee
breaks. The rest was interesting, possibly useful, but definitely in second place to the juicy moments of sharing in the informality of the
coffee breaks. There had to be a better way.

The joke was about *technology*. Ever since that word became
attached to the end of Open Space, strange looks have followed.
How on earth could anything like the Goa experience be called a
technology?

From the viewpoint of strict definition and narrow interpretation,
the word technology is appropriate. There is a *techne* (technique)
involved in order to produce an intended result. But that is stretching
to say the least, and in fact the enterprise was never conceived as a
technology. It was so designated in an odd moment, and the word
just stuck. All of which constitutes a funny story on the way to the
future . . . with a point.

Metaphysical Management and Open Space Technology

At the conclusion of our gathering in Goa, I found myself back in
Bombay with my Indian host, V. S. Mahesh. Mahesh was the vice

president for human resources with the Taj Hotel Group, and we were staying in his palatial establishment, the Taj Bombay.

Mahesh had seen fit to organize a press conference for me with the business writers from the Bombay press, nine gentlemen and one lady. Mahesh did the honors as host and introduced me to the assembled group. In the Indian way, the introduction was quite formal, but its content left me practically speechless.

It seems that a British colleague of mine had just written a book in which four approaches to organizational theory and practice were described, and the last one was characterized as "metaphysical management." It was my privilege to be singled out as the exemplar of this esoteric endeavor. Considering the nature of my work, and what I had been writing about, this characterization was not wholly in error, but definitely not one I would have chosen for myself.

Back to the press conference. My friend Mahesh (I use that term broadly) welcomed the fourth estate and introduced the conference with the words, "This is Harrison Owen, the founder and practitioner of metaphysical management and Open Space Technology. Harrison, would you please explain this and describe what you actually do?"

Eyebrows rose with the mention of metaphysical management, and Mahesh, having pulled off one wonderful oxymoron, could not resist a second. Out came Open Space Technology. Had Mahesh not been a friend, I should certainly have done him bodily harm, and to this day I do not know how seriously he intended his words. But the words had been spoken and I was stuck with them, particularly after the articles came out on the following day, with my name firmly attached to metaphysical management and Open Space Technology.

So that is the story of how Open Space was designated a technology: a fair representation, but not to be taken too seriously. And here's the point. Open Space, from the beginning, required a certain playful appreciation. Taken too seriously, you could be in deep trouble. But as we had discovered in Goa, Open Space works, and for that reason a degree of respect is also in order. Playful respect was, and remains, an essential condition for effective entry into Open Space.

In the beginning, my central, and indeed only, concern was to find a better way for human meeting, which could be at once effective, economic in terms of energy expended, and fun. Perhaps it is the hedonist in me, but I believe that gatherings designed to achieve useful results can only be fully effective when the participants are having fun. The issues on the table, and the implications of the outcomes, may all be deadly serious, but creative interchange, to say nothing of innovative results, seems to disappear quickly when a dark cloud of solemnity hangs over everything.

Inspiration for Open Space

Inspiration for Open Space did not come from an extensive study of meeting management, or organizational dynamics, or the so-called leaderless groups experimented with in the early sixties by the folks at National Training Labs and elsewhere. The point of departure for Open Space was separated from all of the above by thousands of miles and centuries of human experience. It began in Balamah.

Balamah is a very small, unexceptional village in the bush of West Africa. All the residents are Kpelle and they had been in the area for hundreds of years. In more recent time they, along with neighboring tribes, became part of Liberia. Life in Balamah was largely unaffected by this modern national designation, and it was my privilege to spend some extended periods of time in their midst as a guest of the chief.

One of the high experiences for all residents and visitors to the village was the rite of passage for the boys and a similar celebration for the girls. I was fortunate to participate, as much as a Westerner can participate, in both. These celebrations occurred on a seven–year cycle and were replete with complex ritual, pageantry, dance, and just plain fun. Profoundly moving, the renewal of the village was cele-brated as its young people were welcomed to adulthood and acknowledged as the first fruits of the future.

My natural curiosity, to say nothing of a perceived need to be at the right place at the right time, led me to ask what the starting time might be. Blamah, the chief, would just smile and say, "When it's time."

And Blamah was right. The events always started when it was time. But how, I wondered, did anybody know? There were few calendars and such clocks as there were rarely ticked. Even worse, there was no planning committee, and yet the events came off right on schedule, without a hitch. Every time.

Upon reflection, I noticed that several nights prior to the start of either celebration, the drummers in the village did a lot of practicing in the early morning hours. It all seemed rather disorganized, as one drummer announced a short rhythmic phrase that would eventually be answered by a colleague from another quarter of the village. The answer, however, was always some form of elaboration. The rhythmic pattern would be inverted, played backwards, or sometimes started in the middle and played both ways.

Over time, it was as if the village and its drummers were finding their beat, and as the beat settled to some consistent form, the dancers began to appear. First they danced in random groups, or even solo, but gradually the dancers became a dance that circled the perimeter of the village, eventually swirling to the central courtyard, an open space in the heart of the village. As the dancers converged, the rhythm intensified and the festivities began in earnest.

All during the day, dancers and drummers conversed, dancer followed dancer, and sometimes everybody danced. The power of the moment was palpable, and in the dance one could feel the new, emergent spirit of the village made manifest, not only in the presence of the young initiates but most strongly in the total flow of the occasion.

The rhythm waned and the dancers tired. It was almost as if the village collective had been drawing in a deep breath, filling the central open space with life, and then letting that breath out with a pleasant fatigue that bordered on exhaustion. Inspiration, followed by expiration. Life was drawn to the core and then released back to the periphery, as dancers and drummers retired for the night in preparation for another day of celebration.

Simple, beautiful, elegant, organic—Blamah was right; everything began when it was time, and time itself was determined by the rhythmic breathing in and out of the whole village.

I Believe I've Got It!

In the moment, I thought I had the answer to my quest for some effective alternative to gatherings characterized by endless speakers and terminal fanny fatigue, in which the sole bright spots were the coffee breaks. Invite people to join a circle and allow (encourage) that circle to breathe in and out, inspire and expire. Then the spirited interchange, juicy time, just plain fun of the coffee break might re-create itself. Add an equally simple mechanism to identify the substantive issues to be considered, and enable the process of organization in time and space. And there it is: fun and substance!

The bulletin board suggested itself as the *issue raiser,* and the marketplace was an obvious choice for *organizer.* Both the bulletin board and the marketplace are known and used the world over. No explanation is needed and, generally speaking, the mechanisms are so fundamental they can't break.

And there you have it. Four elements create Open Space: circle, breath, bulletin board, and marketplace. The circle creates the conditions of meeting. With that particular geometry, people will get together and communicate, person to person, face to face.

Breath is rather an odd way of talking about what is going on here, but taken metaphorically it points to the organic quality of the Open Space gathering. This is not a mechanical process with gears and shafts, hard surfaces, and wires. Open Space is about life and creating the space in which life can expand, or if you will, breathe.

The bulletin board is one of those wonderful universal phenomena that link human beings. Whether you find yourself in Old Delhi, New York, or plugged into the biggest global bulletin board going, otherwise known as the Internet, the reality is familiar and the rules well known. It's simple: if you have something of concern to you, announce it to the world on the bulletin board.

The marketplace is no less universal or natural. Obviously, many people have written massively about what it is and how it works. Despite their efforts, we all know that we don't know. But isn't it funny? The marketplace just works anyhow. If not here, then there, if not today, then tomorrow, the marketplace, as the environment of human interchange, magically appears whenever folks have something of importance to trade.

Some people talk idly, or seriously, about "controlling the market." We all know, however, that the market is ultimately uncontrollable, and we are reminded of this occasionally when Wall Street suffers meltdown or some other catastrophe. This knowledge has recently been formalized into such wonderful concepts as chaos theory and self-organizing systems, but as every trader of goods or ideas has always known, the marketplace is a living creature of which we were all a part. Subject to its own rules, beholden to no single person, the marketplace is neither more nor less than a potent manifestation of the collective consciousness of Homo sapiens. When invoked in Open Space, the marketplace works its magic by bringing buyers and sellers, users and providers, the knowledgeable and the needful together in an organic tapestry of shared meaning.

With effort, we could have converted our discovery into a hugely complicated and detailed process, replete with manuals and procedural steps. But why bother? It seems that at some innate and deep level, we all know what is going on and how to get along with what's happening. To be sure, some do better than others, but amazingly most people seem to make it most of the time.

Engines of Open Space: Passion and Responsibility

There are two engines powering Open Space: passion and responsibility. For some people the notion of passion is too wild and uncontrollable; they would prefer something like interests or concerns. For myself, I like passion. Anything less just doesn't bring the juices up to a rolling boil, which is absolutely essential if Open Space is going to be other than boring. Open Space begins, and in some ways ends, with the invitation to follow that which has heart and meaning for you. The presumption is that commitment, performance, and excellence only emerge when the heart is engaged meaningfully, and that is called passion.

But passion alone is not sufficient. There must also be responsibility, which will insure that passionate concerns will lead to action. Without responsibility, passion is a flash in the pan, smoke and mirrors, nice ideas, vaporware.

Responsibility alone is insufficient as well. Responsibility without passion is boring, dull, stultifying. It's a real drag. While something useful may get done in the name of duty, duty itself must become the passion or the level of accomplishment will be low.

When passion and responsibility are linked, an opening is created for innovation and something gets done. In Open Space, this translates into excitement and results, or put another way—having fun doing something useful.

Four Principles and One Law

I would love to take credit for enormous foresight and creative powers in the enunciation of the four principles and the one law (the Law of Two Feet). People say that the principles and the law not only make Open Space rich and possible, but they also can be useful guides for daily living. Truth be told, however, all of the above presented themselves as a blinding flash of the obvious. It was what people seemed to be doing anyhow, and the articulation of the principles and the law was merely to acknowledge the experienced reality.

It didn't happen all at once, and I am pretty sure that the first several Open Space events, which were conducted for small experimental groups, never had the benefit of either law or principles formally stated. But by the time we arrived in Goa, five years after the first Open Space event in Monterey, California, in 1985, both elements were very much a part of what we did.

In many ways, the articulation of the principles and the law was a benchmark in the emerging realization of what Open Space could be all about. We noticed, time after time, that the most unlikely people regularly accomplished incredible results, in terms of actions taken or insights achieved. There was no other way to explain what took place except to say: *Whoever comes is the right people.*

The second principle, *Whatever happens is the only thing that could have*, might be construed as pure fatalism, a condemnation to a predetermined universe. The principle, however, is not that complicated, although it may be a lot deeper. At the simplest level, the principle acknowledges the obvious—what is, *is* the only thing present Now. Theoretical possibilities, probabilities, or "shoulds" just don't count. But the truly operative word is *Now*, and the principle opens the way to a deeper perception of Now.

There is no force or prescription here. Nobody has to do anything. But we all live Now, and we might as well get used to it. Living in the past is limiting at best, and living in the future is pure make-believe. Now is all there is. It may be a fleeting instant on the way from the past to the future. Alternatively, Now may be the superbly rich environment, extending infinitely in all dimensions, in which our full potential may be realized. At some level, the choice is ours. The experience of Open Space, almost inevitably, is that Now is stretched past all expectation.

The third principle, *Whenever it starts is the right time*, like the previous ones, is a simple recognition of a surprising fact. In Open Space, clock time doesn't really seem to make all that much difference. The examples are legion, but in one major Open Space event with five hundred people from a cellular phone company, the public address (PA) system was one and one-half hours late in arriving. Needless to say, doing anything useful with that number of people without a PA system was simply out of the question, even though we had only a single day in which to achieve a company-saving turn around. Everybody was quite clear: blowing this opportunity meant kissing the company good-by.

In short, the stakes were excruciatingly high and the PA system was aggravatingly late. Eventually, however, the system arrived and everything worked out just perfectly. With no special effort or outside intervention, scheduled groups rescheduled all by themselves. One might consider this result a rare example of providential intervention, but in fact it is the common experience in Open Space.

We have come to recognize what we should have known all along, clocks set arbitrary limits, and only that. To be sure, our chronometers enable us to fashion the time maps of human experience, the time lines describing past occurrences, and the time projections for coming attractions. But, somehow, things never happened the way we describe them, nor work out the way we expect. Our time maps are like all maps, never to be confused with the territory.

A simple children's joke makes the point. Question: How long does it take to fall over a cliff? Answer: All the rest of your life. A little macabre perhaps, but clearly in critical situations time can be experienced in many ways. On the one hand, the journey envisioned in the joke is a short one, measured in seconds prior to hitting the bottom. Look again and it seems to go on forever as the whole of one's life flashes by, if we are to believe those who have taken the trip and survived to tell the tale.

Near-death experiences apparently have the capacity to wipe out clocks, but they are not the only such phenomena. Lovers recognize that a kiss can last for eternity, and all of us know the timelessness of a clear starry night. It would seem that in most, if not all, significant life experiences, time is an incidental. And what creates the significance? I can only answer: the presence of Spirit, which might also be described as inspired performance or spirited interchange.

Over the several years we have been playing in Open Space, it has become increasingly apparent that the third principle points to the deeper reality. It is all about Spirit as manifest in spirited interchange and inspired performance, which are the hallmarks of Open Space. People quite regularly do what they know to be impossible, and having accomplished that, the rest, whatever that might be, seems much less demanding. Generally speaking, we might assume that such miraculous performance could only be accomplished with tight controls and very careful scheduling. The reality is very often the exact opposite. Performance rises to the extent that people are prepared to dispense with the illusion of control and break the tyranny of the clock.

Visitors to Open Space, whether first timers or old hands, remark on the palpable sense of flow in the environment. High energy, but not frantic, and things really getting done. Clocks, although present, play a relatively minor role in the orchestration of the group. Very quickly there evolves an interior sense of flow that provides the calibration by which the group regulates itself. Clocks are only a convenience (if that), and never the final arbiter.

We have learned, I think, that in the world of Spirit, the world of inspiration and creativity, Now expands effortlessly and without limit. In such a world, time virtually ceases to exist, or perhaps it would be more accurate to say that it starts again with every interjection of Spirit. When there is a new inspiration, a new moment of creativity, a new time begins to be calculated. We speak of "before that moment . . . " and measure our experience "since the break-through . . . " As we say, "Whenever it starts is the right time."

The final principle, *When it's over, it's over*, is once again a blinding flash of the obvious, yet it is a point of obviousness we often over-look. Everything in our experience, and certainly everything in Open Space, has a beginning, a middle, and an end. Ideally, we will cele-brate the beginning and enjoy the middle, but the end is not without its difficulty. It is very hard to let go and move on. At a trivial level, the moving on may be about shifting to another group when the dis-cussion runs dry in the one we joined originally. But somehow this is hard. Politeness, inertia, tradition, all conspire to keep us where we sit.

At a deeper level, the ending may be about a way of doing busi-ness, or about a set of ideas or constructs that have passed their use-fulness. Letting go of that sort of stuff is not without pain, if only because our ego inevitably becomes involved. After all, that was my business, those were my ideas, my constructs. But the truth remains, *When it's over, it's over*. And the only thing to be gained by not moving on is a sense of irrelevance, even failure. Our sense of the Now con-tracts a little, or a lot.

In Open Space, the ending of one thing creates the possibility of the next. When we acknowledge that ending enhances our possibili-ties and increases our space, we expand our Now.

The Law of Two Feet—Personal Freedom and Responsibility

The Law of Two Feet is simple in the extreme. *If at any time you find yourself neither contributing nor learning, use your two feet.* You are a pris-oner of boredom only if you choose to make yourself so. Nobody is responsible for you but you.

The law is simple, but the power and effect are enormous. With a single statement, the great "They" is abolished and personal responsibility is established. No longer is it possible to hold "them" responsible for what you did or didn't do. If you don't like it, if it isn't working for you . . . change it.

With the establishment of personal freedom, and therefore responsibility, the totally voluntary nature of Open Space comes to the fore. Nobody has to be there. Nobody has to do anything. That is the negative way of saying it, but that sort of statement clears a lot of ground from *oughts, shoulds,* and *musts.* With the ground clear, it truly becomes possible to follow that which has heart and meaning.

Somewhere along the line we came up with the absurd notion that if everybody did just what they wanted to, nothing would get done. My experience, and the experience in Open Space, is precisely the opposite. The best way to insure that nothing is done, or that something is done poorly, is to assign the task to somebody who does not care to do it. Seriously, have you ever seen a job done well by somebody who didn't care to do it?

The gifts of the Law of Two Feet do not stop with the introduction of personal responsibility for one's experience. There is also a some-times–not–so–subtle restraining function exercised upon the egotists of the group, those who are sure that they, and they alone, have the "truth," and who are compelled by duty to instruct the less enlightened. Such people (and that undoubtedly includes all of us at some time or another) are real Spirit killers. Their lethal powers, however, are brought quickly to heel when a substantial portion of the group exercises the Law of Two Feet, leaving the enlightened masters talking to themselves. As a matter of fact, just knowing that the captive audience has the freedom to depart at a moment's notice is usually sufficient to keep things flowing in a respectful way.

The law also contributes mightily to the vitality, diversity, and flexibility of the group by creating the conditions of emergence for two wonderful creatures: bumblebees and butterflies. Bumblebees are those people who constantly exercise their freedom to move. Buzzing from group to group, their behavior is anathema to more standard meeting managers, but their contribution is enormous. Bumblebees in Open Space do precisely what bumblebees do in nature: cross-pollinate. Carrying ideas from one point to another, weaving a pattern of meaning from apparently disassociated elements, these creatures enable a surprising level of synergy and creativity.

Butterflies are creatures of a different sort. These are people who may actually never get into a group. Typically they are found sitting under a tree or in the hot tub, or lying by the pool, and the question arises as to why they even bothered to come. With a little observation, however, their contribution becomes apparent. All butterflies have one characteristic in common: they are beautiful. Sooner or later, someone will be attracted and a conversation will begin that never would have happened otherwise. More often than not, the conversation will find its way into the general discussion as a surprising, but nevertheless welcome addition.

Transformation of Conflict: An Unexpected Benefit

One of the least expected and most useful apparent effects of the Law of Two Feet is the transformation of conflict into a positive resource. I say *apparent* because I honestly can't prove a causal connection. It is the case, however, that within Open Space, intensely conflicting issues are engaged without bloodshed and with positive results.

Painful labor/management issues in the corporate world and divisive political and ethnic issues in the world of communities and nations have been worked out in productive and amicable ways, even though the groups were large (from five hundred to eight hundred members), up-front planning time was minimal, and formal conflict resolution procedures were completely absent. In a word, the folks involved basically did it themselves, and having done it themselves once, they are now prepared to handle conflicting situations as they arise in the future.

For example, in a Latin American sugar mill, the shop steward and the plant manager were reported to have been at machete points. Whether true or not, the scenario accurately reflected the state of labor/management relations. Not a happy place. In the course of a single day, meeting under a large tent set in the middle of a bush-whacked cane field, the five hundred managers and workers gathered in Open Space. It was all on the table. Everything. And they talked. By the end of the day, Nirvana had not arrived, but in its place came a new sense of dignity and respect, witness the fact that the shop steward and the plant manager embraced, not perfunctorily, but with real feeling. Something had changed.

How it all works is still very much of a mystery, but I think the Law of Two Feet is critical. With this law, each participant is empowered to participate as much, and as often, as he or she desires. The point is, nobody is coerced into uncomfortable, conflicting situations. But curiously enough, I have never seen anybody leave totally either, even though they were quite at liberty to do so.

Apparently, the initial interest in the subject at hand (creating a better school system, company, or country) creates sufficient magnetic draw to keep people present, while the Law of Two Feet allows them to make the crucial individual decisions about when they have had enough and when they are ready for more. In a word, the people are put "in charge" of their own space. Should they need some breathing space? Take it. Ready for engagement? Do it.

It has become very clear that, given this kind of freedom, folks on the scene can handle enormous issues with minimal assistance—very good news in a fast-moving world brimming with conflict, but without the time, finances, or personnel to mediate every lethal situation.

Something of the mystery in this situation might be removed by taking a leaf from the notebook of the experimental psychologist who discovered that if you put sufficient rats in a small enough cage over an extended period of time, they will kill each other. I suspect that humans, deprived of adequate space, will behave in a similar fashion, although the space need not only be physical space.

The key here is passion, and what happens to passion when it is constrained. We know that Open Space runs on passion; people come because they care. But when one person's passion becomes another's anathema, conflict is the inevitable result—unless sufficient space can be provided.

Faced with conflict, standard practice has been to bring the offending parties together for a negotiated resolution. Doubtless there are times when imminent physical violence warrants such an approach, but I think it important to recognize that something is also lost in this practice, and that is passion and the results that specific passions can produce. In the name of preserving order, and most usually the *established order*, we eliminate conflict. But what about those situations where it is the established order itself that needs to be eliminated? Or if not eliminated then radically altered and/or expanded? Our standard practices effectively remove the engine of change.

Implicit in our actions is the presumption that we *know* how things ought to work, but supposing we don't know, or that our knowledge is based on a very limited view of the possible. Questions such as these have an academic ring about them, but they quickly become real in the world of our present experience, where today's way of doing business is an almost certain prescription for going out of business tomorrow. We need passion and the gifts that passion can bring—creativity and innovation.

The experience of Open Space suggests another way. In the presence of conflict, simply open more space and allow the imprisoned passion to run free, creating the objects of its desire. Talk about being out of control! But somehow every group I have worked with has had the collective wisdom and the capacity to learn and grow from virtually any stimulus. Stated bluntly, I have never seen any situation, no matter how full of conflict and passion laden, where apparent outrage and potential violence could not be turned to positive advantage. To be sure, the anxiety levels of the sponsors and the participants, to say nothing of the facilitator, showed every indication of going off the scale. But it worked—*provided* that more space was opened.

It is important to understand that space is not just physical space, which is definitely limited, at least on this planet. Indeed, space comes in a variety of flavors, which we might call *virtual space,* or *psychic space,* and probably some others. The Westernized, technological world has recently become mesmerized with virtual space in the form of the Internet. Cyberspace, by whatever name, appears as a new unending frontier. Talk about controlling it is almost laughable, for that which has neither beginning nor end can scarcely be contained and controlled. In a word, there is plenty of space here for passion and creativity to run amuck, very positively. And when con-flict appears, just open more space.

Psychic space provides another venue for expansion. This is an uncomfortable arena for many in the West, and indeed some will deny its existence. But for other peoples and places, psychic space, or what we might call inner space, is critical and also unending.

As a sometime visitor to India, I am always impressed with how so many people seem to get along so well in such close proximity. There are problems, and sometimes bloody ones, resolved in a way that many of us would find unacceptable, but every day something close to one billion Indians muddle through, and even seem to enjoy it.

Americans would never make it, but I think the significant dif-ference is the Indian recognition that physical space is only one form of space, and probably not the most important one. With five thousand years of experience and hard work, our friends on the subcontinent have gotten rather good at exploring their interior environments, which they perceive to have no limits. Under the cir-cumstances, there is plenty of room for differences, passions of all sorts, and while conflicts certainly arise, there is usually room to work around them.

It would be reasonable to ask what are the limitations on the use of Open Space in a situation full of conflict. From personal experi-ence, I don't know of too many. I would insist with some groups that they leave weapons outside, but other than that I have yet to encounter a group of people or a set of issues where Open Space would not make a positive, substantive contribution. The Law of Two Feet seems to provide the space required. Of course, this does not mean that Open Space is appropriate to every situation.

Indications and Contraindications for Use

Four factors create the appropriate conditions for Open Space. They do not all have to be present, but the more factors in evidence the better the results. The factors are

- high levels of complexity, in terms of issues to be dealt with;
- high levels of diversity, in terms of the folks who have to work the issues;
- high levels of conflict (actual or potential);
- a decision needed yesterday.

Open Space *should not be used* when the end result is predetermined. If you already know the precise nature of the issues involved and (within reasonable tolerances) what should be done about them, using Open Space is not only a waste of time, it will probably backfire. Open Space does what it says: it creates an open environment. Should it turn out that the environment is really closed and the answers are in and known, then the people involved will feel (justifiably) used and abused. In short, they will not be happy.

All of which brings up the most critical issue regarding the use/nonuse of Open Space: *control.* Organizations over the past fifty years (at least) have been based on the notion that somebody is actually in charge, somebody is in control. Indeed, we tend to measure our performance in terms of how well control is exercised. If you are out of control, typically you are out of a job. In Open Space, the rules are rather different. *If you are in a control mode, think you are in control, or want to be in control, Open Space is not for you, and you are not for Open Space.*

Open Space as a Journey

By now you will understand that life with Open Space has been an ongoing process of discovery. We first experienced a rather different way of being together, and then sought to articulate and enhance the experience.

Now that Open Space has grown up, as it were, it might seem appropriate to clean up our act in terms of the articulation of the four principles and the one law. As many people have pointed out, they are questionable grammatically, and definitely on the folksy side. I doubt that such a cleanup will ever take place. First, because the principles and the law seem to work as stated. And if it ain't broke, don't fix it. A second and deeper reason is that Open Space is fundamentally "of and for the people," so if the language sounds folksy, that's as intended. But nothing is ever set in concrete, and as people use Open Space the words change. This is especially true when Open Space moves out of an English environment. I can't remember how you state the principles in French, German, Spanish, or Hindi. But one thing is for sure, they look nothing like what I am familiar with. I am told, however, that when the language becomes too formal, something of the Spirit is lost.

Critical Elements of Open Space

The journey of discovery is by no means over, for every day we unearth new insights and opportunities, some of which are reported in the next chapter. But before moving onward, allow me to offer a brief summary of the critical elements and principles of Open Space as they stand at the moment.

The Four Mechanisms

- Circle
- Breath
- Bulletin Board
- Marketplace

The Four Principles

- Whoever comes is the right people.
- Whatever happens is the only thing that could have.
- Whenever it starts is the right time.
- When it's over, it's over.

The One Law

- If at any time during our time together you discover that you are neither learning nor contributing, use your two feet and move on.

The Four Conditions for Use

- High levels of complexity
- High levels of diversity
- High potential or actual conflict
- A decision time of yesterday

Two Engines to Drive With

- Passion
- Responsibility

Chapter III

Open Space on the Loose:
The Now Grows

*O*pen Space has spread around the world. While definitive numbers are impossible to obtain and the evidence is largely anecdotal, there have been major applications on every continent, in a wide range of settings, and with varying numbers of participants. Open Space has been used effectively with groups ranging from five to over one thousand members, involving multiple cultures, languages, industries, political persuasions, sexual preferences, ethnicities, economic levels, and educational achievement. Corporations, governments, school systems, religious institutions, ecosystems (watersheds), hospitals, mental health facilities, drug abuse organizations, third world villages, and rural cooperatives have all found a home in Open Space. Conservative guesstimates suggest that thousands of events have involved tens and probably hundreds of thousands of participants.

The spread of Open Space has occurred in a surprisingly short time frame. The first event of any sort occurred in 1985. The first event with "real people" occurred in 1989 (Goa). For the next two years (until 1992), I and several others were essentially the only "practitioners," and our practice might have included five events per year, at the outside.

The rate of dissemination is even more remarkable because on the face of it, Open Space appears a highly unlikely candidate to spread at all. Established theory and practice in the area of meeting management and general organizational behavior are apparently violated to the point that Open Space seems counterintuitive at best, and probably just plain wrong. It is a fact. Every single group that I have worked with, anywhere in the world, has always said, in one way or another, "Harrison, this is a wonderful idea, but it simply will not work with this group."

It is impossible to fault those who hold such opinions, for there is little in their prior experience or education to suggest that Open Space could be effective. And frankly, had I not had the experience of the past twelve years, I would feel precisely the same way. Inviting large numbers of cantankerous, diverse, conflicted individuals to work on hugely complex issues, without enormous effort devoted to agenda preparation and without an army of facilitators, seems to be a sure and certain prescription for disaster. This is precisely what Open Space does, and despite the skepticism, Open Space works.

It might also be noted that the dissemination of Open Space has taken place without benefit of corporate sponsorship, marketing budgets and personnel, or even the semblance of a plan. It has been the practice just to give it away. To be sure, there are now books and training programs, all of which emerged because there was neither the time nor the energy to give the gift of Open Space to one person at a time. But Open Space is there for anyone who chooses to use it.

Some of my colleagues have wondered why no attempt was made to trademark or franchise the operation. From the beginning, Open Space has not been a proprietary product. No person, least of all me, owns the rights.

The reasons are very practical. First, the process is so simple that anybody with a good head and a good heart can "do" it. It is true that training and experience will raise the level of practitioner competency, but creating Open Space seems to be a natural act. We can all do it, if we choose to.

There is a deeper reason no trademark or franchise was ever contemplated. Open Space Technology was not available for trademark or franchise. Open Space is the birthright of every person on the planet. It need only be claimed. Creating space, expanding our Now is, so far as I am concerned, what the human journey is all about. We all own the rights.

Open Spaces and Places

The short life of Open Space has provided diverse experiences in application. More interesting than the actual numbers involved has been the range of situations in which the approach has been applied. It is curious, however, that in each situation, no matter how widely it may vary from other situations, the actual dynamics are virtually identical. It makes little difference whether the group consists of twenty–five or seven hundred and fifty, is from the East or the West, contains Ph.D.'s or marginally literate villagers, Open Space works the same way, and what I described as taking place in Goa has been replicated again and again. The details of the conversation and the concrete results may be as different as night and day, but the *affective* results are so similar that one would be hard pressed to differentiate groups based upon their observed behavior. In other words, engineers will produce engineering and villagers will produce plans for their village, but in each case the common experience involves feelings of high energy, synergy, productivity, and fun.

A Swedish friend of mine said he finally figured out Open Space. He called it the WD–40 (a marvelous universal solvent) of group work. One shot will loosen up just about anything.

I think that is a bit of an overstatement, as there are some situations where Open Space does not work well, as we have noted. But the truth of the matter is that Open Space works…often very well and usually with surprising results.

The Stories of Open Space

Fully telling the tales of Open Space is an impossible task, and certainly that is true within the constraints of this book. The following sketches are almost a random sample, providing something of the flavor and diversity.

Olympics Bound

The Olympics are a big deal, and also a big business, particularly if you happen to be a major corporate sponsor. The stakes are high and the rewards potentially enormous. It is all about doing good and doing well at the same time, in terms of exposure to the world public.

AT&T plays in this game for reasons both altruistic and bottom line. Their contribution: a major pavilion in the Global Village. Their design team for the Summer 1996 Olympics was not your everyday gathering of folks. Alongside a minimal number of AT&T executives, there were to be found such people as the woman who had done all the lighting for Grateful Dead concerts and the person who had done the special effects for the movie *Apollo 13*. For ten months, this crew labored intently, finally producing a satisfactory design. Longer than a football field and costing more than a few million dollars, this surrealistic contribution to the Global Village of the '96 Olympics was ready for construction. But there was a small problem and a major opportunity. Actually, the opportunity was the problem.

The Olympic Committee was so pleased with the AT&T effort that they made an offer no corporation could refuse: please move your pavilion from the edge of the Global Village to dead center. Talk about exposure! But that was the problem.

On the edge of the village, AT&T might anticipate five thousand visitors a day, a number their design could well handle. In the center, the visitor flow would increase overwhelmingly to seventy-five thousand per day, minimum. In one instant, a wonderful design, which took ten months to create, went straight out the window. Worse than that, if they took ten months to create a new design, everything would be ready to go only well after the Summer Olympics were history.

Enter Open Space. Just a week after the corporate moguls had made their decision, the design team, all twenty-three of them, gathered to make meaning and opportunity out of an enormous mess. The team was not happy. Not only had their hard work been thrown out the window, but the time available to put something new together was something less than optimal. To top it all off, Russ Natoce, the AT&T executive responsible, proposed using some weird new process where there was no predetermined agenda and people were encouraged to do just what they wanted to. Obviously, disaster was about to turn into total catastrophe.

It was indeed a skeptical crew assembled in the circle. They were angry because their plan had been rejected, even though the reasons might be good ones. They were concerned, or let's say it as it was, frightened . . . because they all knew there was no way, doing things as they had always been done, that they could have a workable design in time for the Olympics. That is where we started.

By five o'clock on the second day, or thirty-six hours from start, there was a collective smile on twenty-three faces. They had all done what they knew to be totally impossible, and best of all the design that emerged was better (as agreed by all) than the old one. While there had been lots of intensity, conflict converted into breakthrough, giving birth to rich ideas and practical application. Disaster became opportunity, transforming to creation, and it had all been fun.

And the bottom line remained the bottom line. When you compress ten months of design effort on a multimillion dollar project into two days, emerge with a better product, and have all the participants still talking to each other, that is known as competitive advantage, the stuff from which real profits are made.

Joining the Mainstream

In Saint Catharines, a city in Ontario, Canada, a socially conscious group known as MainStream Access provides shelter and support for developmentally challenged individuals. In late 1992, the management team of this organization attended a workshop to learn the ways of Open Space. Returning to their organization, they tried it out, and the results were not only different but also better than anybody would have anticipated.

The invitees to the first MainStream Open Space were the staff of counselors and other support people who ran the residential centers for the clients. The focal theme was improving the quality of their operation. Because money is always an issue with such a group, the event took place in one of the centers.

Off they went, and Open Space happened just according to the plan, which of course didn't exist. Not included in the plan was the fact that the clients, who were living in the center used for the event, understandably thought it would be alright if they joined in the festivities, which they did.

The results were gratifying, if not surprising. Contrary to what one might have expected, the clients had absolutely no problem in Open Space. Indeed, they made major contributions, which could even be measured in hard numbers. Two years after the process began, the agency was serving twice the number of clients with no increase in budget. That is a 100 percent increase in productivity. And how did they do that? It turns out that a substantial portion of the services the agency had been providing to its clients were neither needed nor wanted, but nobody ever asked the clients. In Open Space, the clients seized the moment and set the record straight. With fewer services needed and supplied, more clients could be served.

There was another result that I think could be even more significant. The clients who participated in the Open Space began to show an increased ability to cope in the world. Open Space was never designed as a therapeutic intervention, but that it should have therapeutic effect is not a total surprise. When people are treated with respect and expected to take responsibility for their actions—as they are in Open Space—they usually respond positively. The clients in question did no less, which enabled them to do more.

There's More to Doors . . .

For most people, doors are rather prosaic. Something to go in and out of, but scarcely an object of passionate concern. But most people are not engineers at the Boeing Company's Commercial Aircraft Group, for whom doors are more than a matter of idle curiosity. As a matter of fact, doors and the manufacture of same are matters of professional livelihood for more than twenty thousand people, located all over the world, who are responsible for the way in and out of six different airplanes (the 727s through the 777s).

Making a door that will withstand the pressures, temperature changes, and constant abuse experienced by the standard commercial airliner is a complex task, made even more so by competitive pressures that demand costs be driven down. Just to make things more difficult, door components are manufactured all over the world by different national companies who were fortunate to profit from Boeing's largesse, created by the "buy local" program. National airlines sometimes stipulate that some components of the airplanes they buy be made within their national boundaries. Quite understandable, but productive of a quality control and coordination headache of major proportions.

And while you are savoring that head-banger, consider the following. Senior management mandated a strategic plan for the entire door value chain (all the people and products that go into the manufacture of doors), to be completed in less than two months. Not only are the people located all over the place, but the technology of door making is dispersed through multiple heads, with no one person, or even a small group, possessing the entire picture. Putting together such a plan would be a monster of complexity, rendered infinitely confusing by the very narrow time constraints.

So how about getting everybody who cares about doors together in virtual space, in addition to physical space? After all, Open Space and cyberspace are pretty much the same sort of thing, and the Internet is clearly the biggest Open Space going.

The Boeing solution was simultaneous, multisite Open Space, connected online. Two hundred people, representing all aspects of the door value chain, gathered in Seattle, Washington, and Wichita,

Kansas. At each site, they identified the issues and opportunities for building better doors, created discussion groups, and set to work identifying the strategic elements and ways to deal with them. As each group concluded, they entered the results of their discussion online, creating instant proceedings and making them available to their colleagues at the other site. Common issues from the several sites were combined, and at the end of two days a composite report was created, printed over night, and made available in both places on the morning of the third day. An electronic balloting procedure enabled the group to collectively prioritize all of the issues.

At the end of two and one-half days, all parties had been heard from and the rudiments of a strategic plan existed. Was it pretty? No, but the basis had been laid to make it so. With the major elements identified, discussed, prioritized, and documented by the very people who knew the most and had the most at stake, it remained only to fine-tune the information and prepare a pretty document. Here was a strategic plan that was not going to gather dust on the shelf. It represented marching orders to the people who had to march, created by the marchers themselves.

As so often happens in the corporate environment, priorities change and yesterday's plan is set aside for more pressing business. In the case of Boeing, the Door Plan never happened because it was subsequently decided (at least for the moment) to outsource (contract out) virtually all door production. But all was not lost, for the planning efforts in fact became helpful for the orientation of the new contractor. There were other gains as well, if not to organizational effectiveness, then at least to the Spirit of the place, as witnessed by this unsolicited comment from one of the participants.

Note to the Door Product Planning Team

I would just like to say:

From my position at the bottom of the chain (door mechanic), I would first like to thank you for the chance to participate in this process. I feel that I have more to contribute than just building or rigging the doors. You have made it possible to do so.

We have discussed many valuable topics, valuable not only because they deal with the issues from continuing business today—but also valuable because they deal with Boeing's future.

On a personal level, this type of format allows me to interact with others who have a common goal, which is to help preserve the future of Boeing, which in turn allows me to preserve my family's future.

I believe that Boeing can use this format in many if not all areas of the company.

Thank you again!
James J. Queen

For the Love of Canada

How about inviting a whole country for an Open Space? It sounds pretty outrageous, and probably a lot of people would not come, but it certainly is an idea to conjure with.

The outrageous became reality in Canada following the recent referendum in which the residents of Quebec voted by the narrowest of margins to remain a part of the nation. Even though the union was secure for the moment, the issue of Canada's essence and destiny was now irrevocably on the table. Feelings ran high in all quarters, and conversation, such as it was, ran to the polemical.

A Canadian friend remarked, "Even if we are going to divorce, wouldn't it be wise to talk a bit first?" Similar questions obviously occurred independently, and simultaneously, in a number of places, and for a small band of people the answer was quite simple: let's try a little Open Space.

At inception, the plan was nonexistent. There was no coordinated, national effort to open spaces across the country. There were just individuals resolved to create a little safe space in which needed conversation about the future of a land they loved might take place. Chris Carter in Vancouver, Myriam Laberge in Delta, Eleanor Belfry-Lytle in Amherstview, Birgitt Bolton in Ancaster, Larry Peterson in Toronto, Joan DeNew in Hamilton, and more . . . lots more . . . all creating space in which the reality of Canada might be appreciated and grown. Past the narrow rhetoric of some politicians, beyond the sound bites of national television, it was all about the candid conversations of common citizens, following that which had heart and meaning. Now was expanding exponentially.

And it grew. *Macleans Magazine* did a story and then hosted an online conversation for Canadian cybernauts. The Canadian

Broadcasting Company got into the act when it put two of the co-conspirators on the evening news live and coast to coast. Even the prime minister and his deputy dipped their toes into Open Space when they agreed to accept "the book," a product of forty-plus Open Space events and multiple online conversations all across Canada. The title said it all, *For the Love of Canada: A Work in Progress*.

Did it do any good? Well, if you mean, was Canada saved? we will have to wait a bit to see. But the conversation was definitely opened up, and most importantly it was opened up at the citizen level. Common people started doing uncommon things, and it continues. The book was presented to the prime minister, but most importantly Open Space keeps popping up all over, most recently in a proposal for a simultaneous, multisite event in Vancouver and Montreal. Will it happen? Who knows, but the meaning of citizen participation and participatory democracy is taking on some new dimensions.

Expanding Our Now: A Work in Progress

The diversity of the examples is obvious, but the common bond may be less so: it is the continual expansion of Now. With the AT&T Olympic project example, you can almost attach numbers to the enlarged Now. All the participants in that project knew at the start that to do what they proposed to do would take ten months, based upon their prior experience. And then magic happened, or that is how Russ Natoce described it. What should have taken ten months was accomplished in two days. When two days expands to include all the energy and accomplishment of ten months, you have a pretty big Now on your hands.

The folks at Mainstream discovered their Now expanding along a number of vectors. Doubtless the most profound was the inclusion of the gifts, contributions, and humanity of Mainstream's clients in the management's "present reality" (otherwise known as Now). A bifurcated Now became whole, or at least began the process of becoming whole, as the distinction between client and staff began to dissolve in the safe space of Open Space.

As the organization achieved wholeness, Now expanded along another vector. It is called doubling your money, or what amounts to the same thing: using the same amount of budget for twice the impact. With that sort of expanded Now, feelings of scarcity rapidly convert to a deep experience of abundance.

The folks at Boeing experienced an expanded Now by bringing into awareness all the component skills, interests, contributions, and stakeholders of the "kingdom of doors." On an average working day, most folks saw no further than the end of their next task. Looking neither to the right nor the left, they plowed onward. There is a certain admirable, gritty determination in such an approach, but the net effect is a real skinny Now. There is also a genuine fear of everything that is not Now: all those other people doing different but unseen and unknown things. As everything and everybody are brought into the light, as one big conversation develops, fear mitigates and Now expands. It turns out that there are lots of brothers and sisters on the journey together.

And what can be said about those Canadians? Are they creating a big Now, or what? Holding a whole country in your consciousness is a stretch, but that is the stuff out of which genuine community is made. Needless to say, Canada has not been saved, and it may never be; however, the Now created in the minds, hearts, and souls of all those who are participating will never be forgotten. It will always add value to whatever the future discussions may bring.

After Open Space—What?

Presently there is no such thing as long–term experience with Open Space, for it has only been in the past several years that anything approaching a significant number of applications has been achieved, and the subsequent period of time is way too short for definite conclusions. Recently, two institutes have been established, one in Canada and one in the United States, in order to capture, analyze, and disseminate the Open Space experience. There are, however, some early returns that may be pointing the way.

The first item, which almost everybody notices, is that in the time period immediately following an Open Space event, there appears to be a subtle spread of Open Space principles, if not the method itself. This shows up in the words that people use in the course of their everyday meetings. When things go on too long, with little productive result, it is not uncommon to hear something like, "I'm exercising the Law of Two Feet," or "When it's over, it's over." To the extent that these words are acted upon, and I can't say how often that is, there has occurred a marked shift from previous standard behavior.

Less common, but still in evidence, is the actual migration of the Open Space approach across the system. At USWest, an American telephone company, for example, after an Open Space event was held in Arizona, self–initiated events took place in other widely scattered areas throughout the company.

The Bank of Montreal (BOM) had a similar experience, and indeed Open Space now seems to be a part of regular operations in some areas. In at least one of their regions, they have used Open Space on a number of occasions to deal with the process of rationalizing their business and bringing in new branches. The impact of Open Space also seems to have been felt in everyday life. In what seems like a small incident, BOM executives decided that they liked meeting in a circle, Open Space style, without the standard conference table. Hence they did away with the mahogany monster in their conference room. Most folks, apparently, did not pay that much attention to the change in decor until one day when they were forced to meet in borrowed space that came with table. Participants testify that it was the worst meeting they had ever had, and now all tables are gone.

Sometimes the impact of Open Space is not quite what one would expect. An American corporation fired its CEO because, even though he had initiated the use of Open Space, he refused to follow up on the results in the manner of Open Space. This wasn't about substance but style, and when this individual began to micromanage with a vengeance, it seems that the Law of Two Feet came into play, or at least some version of it.

At this point, few organizations have thought to try Open Space on a continuing basis. A few have, however, and one of them is the Wesley Urban Ministry in Hamilton, Ontario. This organization's mission is to serve all those who are not served by anyone else: the abused, the homeless, and the addicted. The executive director, Birgitt Bolton, came to an Open Space training program and then tried Open Space with her staff. She was surprised later when her staff approached her with what seemed like an ultimatum—they didn't want any more Open Space events; they wanted to work in Open Space all the time.

Inasmuch as nobody had ever quite done that before, it took a little getting used to. After all, if everybody does just what they want to, what can possibly get done. As it turned out, a lot. Topping the list was the fact that two years after taking the plunge, the organization was offering twice the services with a 10 percent smaller budget. Not only that, their employee retention rate went up, apparently due to the fact that people felt respected and actually enjoyed what they were doing.

Life at Wesley was not without its bumps and pitfalls, and Birgitt chronicles these in a wonderful essay to be found in *Tales from Open Space* (Abbott Publishing, 1995). But the biggest bump was the reaction of the board of directors. They were sure that Birgitt was out of control, and in spite of the obvious success of the venture, forced her out of her position. But the story doesn't end there, I am happy to say. One year later, Birgitt was named Woman of the Year by the city of Hamilton, and much of the board has been encouraged to use its energies elsewhere. As for Birgitt, she is busily creating a new career for herself as an organizational consultant, and Open Space is very much a part of her practice. So far as I know, Open Space is alive and well, living in Hamilton.

It is probably safe to say that Open Space is not for the faint hearted, and certainly not an approach to be used lightly. But as far as I am concerned, the results are tending in a positive direction. We will have to see how it all turns out.

Open Space as Part of Larger Interventions

Hugh Huntington, an independent consultant working with Honey–well AreoSpace, had an interesting challenge. With the outbreak of peace, priorities shifted both radically and quickly in the defense industry. Hugh's job was to assist in the downsizing of Honeywell's aerospace division from roughly twenty–eight hundred people to something like twelve hundred people, in a very short period of time. The details of this particular adventure may also be found in *Tales from Open Space* (Abbott Publishing, 1995), but briefly, Hugh used a series of Open Space events across the entire organization to allow people to redesign the division themselves and then implement their design. Not only did they meet their objectives, but the participants reported that it had been a profoundly moving experience in a posi–tive way. One of the most remarkable effects was the apparent absence of the so–called "survivor syndrome."

Open Space as the Intervention

There are a number of examples of Open Space being used in ways similar to Hugh Huntington's experience with Honeywell, but an emerging realization on the part of my colleagues and myself is that the Open Space event itself can become the intervention. This is because it is in the nature of an Open Space event for participants to experience fundamental shifts of understanding, relationship, and modes of work. There is always the question of how long these shifts will last or how far they will go. We have learned some about extending the impact, but we still have a lot to learn, and the people involved always know that something important happened. In this way, the Open Space experience becomes a story of the possible. What happened once could happen again; a new benchmark of per–formance has been established.

Before and After Open Space

Even though the long–term results of Open Space are far from in, it is quite clear that the impact of an event upon an organization can be considerable. Preparing an organization to deal with that impact prior to the event is essential, and working with them afterward to maximize the benefits only makes sense.

In general, the results of an Open Space event are positive, opening the door to enhanced organizational function. The results may also be surprising, and in some cases unpleasantly so: witness the CEO who found it necessary to seek alternate employment. There is probably no way to eliminate the surprises, but it should be possible to eliminate the surprise of surprise. It is my practice to post a large sign during the event, "Be Prepared to Be Surprised," and to go over that little piece of advice with the sponsoring group before we get into the thick of things.

Working with the group afterward is also important to insure that full advantage has been taken of the new possibilities. Open Space is always more than the event itself, which means that by intent or happenstance, it is part of a bigger picture.

Chapter **IV**

What on Earth Is Going On?

*O*pen space is a strange phenomenon. It works even though much of what we have all been taught, and presume to know, says that it should not. The obvious question is, why?

A possible image of an organization, or meeting, is that of a her–metically sealed box with several closely guarded points of entrance and egress. If we are to believe the reports of many executives, who see life as an unending succession of meetings, the difference between a meeting and the organization may be fundamentally a matter of size. In any event, this box is called a "closed system." Clearly defined walls separate the inside from the outside, and police persons (known as managers or "those in charge") both defend the connections to the world beyond and insure decorous and productive behavior within.

Much time is devoted to the articulation of structure, and those who perform that function, called senior executives, are accorded a mixture of fear and awe. They give. They take away. With the stroke of a pen, whole divisions, departments, subsidiaries suddenly emerge or disappear.

The fixation on structure is extended over time by an equivalent fixation on planning. The operation of the structure is projected into the future with detailed instructions as to who will do what, where, when, and how. And God forgive those who do not have a plan and follow it.

Overstatement? Certainly, but probably not too far from the operational picture that many of us have inside our heads as we go to work, attend meetings, or engage in a variety of community activities. Obviously (and thankfully), the world of work does not completely match this forbiddingly sterile picture. Things are messier, but we can see the ideal. One of these days, we'll get organized, have a plan, get in control of things. And then...

And then, the kingdom of God, nirvana, or whatever the current picture of perfection might be called, will surely have arrived. Life will be predictable, employment will go on forever, and job satisfaction will progress inexorably from good to better to best. In the twinkling of an eye, our career plans and our strategic plans will have been met. Not exceeded, mind you, but met. To exceed the plan would mean planning error, and that would mean lack of control. God forbid we should get out of control.

And there is the rub (to paraphrase Shakespeare). The world in which we do business is very hard on those who see control as the beginning, middle, and end of all that is meaningful. Col. George Norwood, who was in charge of planning for some part of the U. S. military at the time of the Gulf War, was quoted in the *Washington Post* as saying, "All of a sudden the world changed, and it didn't match what we were planning on." Surprise, George, but what did you expect?

With a control model of organization, life becomes progressively difficult, as expectations and present experience diverge. Not all the shocks to our organizational concept, however, are necessarily bad. Case in point is Open Space and the curious fact that it works. Human beings have the demonstrated capacity to get things done in an environment marked by the lack of predetermined agendas and structures, rigidly defined boundaries, and designated individuals responsible for the orderly progress of affairs. This is not a singular phenomenon, but one that is happening again and again, in all corners of the globe, with an amazing variety of the sorts and conditions of humankind. What on earth, we might ask, is going on?

Open Space Is Not the Exception?

An outrageous thought comes to mind. Suppose that the Open Space experience is not, as it might appear, the exception, but rather the rule. Not some fantasm, but the way things are. Under these circumstances, the appearance of Open Space is not an aberration but rather a breakthrough of reality. The aberration lies with our concept of what organizational life should be like.

In a word, we might be shooting ourselves in the foot. The world may not be as we have conceptualized it, and any similarity between our concept and reality may be purely coincidental. Open Space, it could turn out, is simply the way things are, and if we are stressing out, attempting to rationalize the world of our experience with our concept of control, we are wasting our time and causing ourselves no small amount of needless pain and anxiety. Better to let go and enjoy. Doubtless this is heresy, but it might be a way to go.

Open Systems/Closed Systems

Several years ago I found myself in Bombay attending a symposium on "Time." For reasons too complex to enumerate, many of the presentations and much of the discussion revolved around the newly emerging field of chaos/complexity theory. As I sat watching videos of cloud patterns manifesting the fractal signature of chaos at work, I was overwhelmed by what I felt to be a profound realization: *Every-thing is connected, nothing stands in splendid isolation.* Systems merging, new systems emerging, everything interpenetrating and influencing everything else, all at a level of complexity that simply numbs the human mental capacity to track the details, let alone think about them. In that instant, the notion of a closed system died for me.

The loss was not without a degree of trauma, for over the course of my entire professional life I had never questioned what I took to be an indisputable fact: the existence of both open systems and closed systems. My understanding was that open systems admitted influence from a host of external factors, while closed systems were effectively shielded from the external environment, and therefore free to operate according to their own internal rules.

An open system was uncontrollable by definition, for just as everything appeared to be in order, an errant variable from the out-side world might impinge upon the stable reality and send it off in a new direction. A closed system was just the opposite, a perfect model of order and control, which once established, continued within the parameters of its initial design.

Given a choice, there was absolutely no question as to which type of system people would prefer, particularly if they were in the busi-ness of running an organization. A closed system offered control and that translated into efficiency, effectiveness, and profitability. Who could argue with "the system"?

Within a closed system, the job of the manager or executive was definable and clear cut: structure the system, assign authority and responsibility, protect the boundaries, and above everything else, maintain control. Do all these things and you too will inherit the kingdom.

But if there is no such thing as a closed system, the organizational environment becomes a rather different affair. For openers, control, as we think we have it, simply does not exist. Doing business as we say we are doing business quickly becomes an exercise in futility and frustration.

There is, of course, a way out. If everybody is convinced that there really is such a thing as a closed system, and all act as if it were so, the fiction might be maintained. There are certain obvious advantages to such a strategy, not the least of which is that when somebody else is in charge, I don't have to be, and as a consequence I am not accountable for what happens.

The Emperor Is Naked

If all of this sounds vaguely reminiscent of the old story about the emperor's clothes, the connection is not coincidental. As long as everybody said that the emperor was fully garbed, that's the way it was. As long as we collectively maintain the belief that closed systems truly exist, and act as if they do, we can probably get away with it, as in fact we have. Certainly there are some chinks in the armor, apparent to everybody, but if the holes can be taken as exceptions that prove the rule, we are in good shape. Or so it seems, and so it has been for a number of years.

One might reasonably ask how we got into this situation in the first place, for obviously suggestions of mass delusion and a conspiracy of silence warrant some explanation. My best guess is that it was one of those theories that seemed to make sense at the time, and once accepted has been hard to let go of.

The notion of a closed system started in the physical sciences as a conceptual means for controlling variables. This is a complicated way of saying that if you are running an experiment, it is important to know that you are looking at what you think you are looking at and not at something else, which may have sneaked in. In order to achieve this controlled state (it's called a controlled experiment), you "close the system."

Closing the system is partially a physical act, so for example, if you are experimenting with radiation, you construct walls of lead to block ambient radiation that might throw off your calculation. But closing the system is also an act of faith, or what amounts to the same thing. You act *as if* the system were closed, and hope that such stray neutrons or quarks as may filter through will fall below the threshold of disturbance that could affect your experiment. But as a scientist, you have always known that a closed system is an intellectual fabrication, created to aid the experimental process. There has never existed an actual closed system, except in your mind.

At the point of invention, and used within careful limits, the twin notions of a closed system and controlled variables are very useful. But somehow what started out as an acknowledged fabrication, useful in certain circumstances, turned into "the truth." Exactly how this occurred, I am not sure, but the following story may offer a likely explanation.

In the early days of behavioral science, the precursor and parent of management science, there was no small effort devoted to achieving legitimacy in the eyes of the scientific community. The way forward appeared to lie in the adoption of the same degree of rigor as is found in the physical sciences, which of course included such things as controlled variables and closed systems. The struggle for legitimacy was by no means easy, nor is it over, as I discovered during a three-year stint at the National Institutes of Health (NIH). Everybody at NIH knows that real science is hard science, physical science. All the rest (sociology, psychology, and so on) are "witchcraft" (to quote a senior cardiovascular physiologist).

Somewhere along the way from hard science to behavioral science to management science, things got a little mixed up. What started out as an arbitrary but nevertheless useful concept, somehow became the bastion of truth itself and the pillar upon which all else is built. But every hard scientist worth his or her salt has always known that nobody ever actually controls an experiment, you just try like the devil and ultimately pretend. The notion of closing a system in a laboratory is marginally thinkable. The same notion is totally absurd when applied to the world we live in, home of an infinitude of space and multiplicity of species, all interacting.

The movement from laboratory to boardroom can be seen as curious, and at some level pathetic, if it were to turn out that tight control, being in charge, and all those other things beloved in the executive suite, depend upon the flawed application of the notion of the closed system. We would then have to face the fact that nobody has that sort of control, simply because there is no such thing as a closed system, and there never has been.

Muddling Through

Despite everything, we have managed to muddle through. We have given birth to a level of productivity and a standard of physical life previously unknown on the planet. Technology flourishes and the wonders of science abound. Whether all of this was based upon a delusion or not, it seems to have worked.

I think the truth of the matter is that our notion of closed systems and tight control worked (or seemed to work) in a slower time, which has now definitely passed us by. In the good old days, when there were fewer of us, doing less, at a slower pace, and with marginal communication, we could maintain the illusion of walls and isolation, combined with the ultimate illusion of control. We had the luxury of "heading West" to the land of open spaces and splendid isolation. At least that is what we did in the United States. Other peoples went in other directions to follow the manifest destiny of expanding colonial empires. Either way, you could travel for months and never see a soul, and it took the same amount of time for news to return. No wonder we could believe in the possibility of closed systems and tight control, because that is the way it was, effectively, if not in fact.

If, however, we look a little more closely at what worked and how, the picture shifts a bit. First of all, it doesn't take a doomsday analyst to understand that it is precisely our level of productivity that has occasioned massive levels of toxic waste, otherwise known as environmental pollution. As far as I know, nobody really doubts that continuing to do business as we have done business is to throw Homo sapiens out of business. The planet itself will doubtless endure, as will many other species, but we will surely be in some difficulty.

Toxic waste, however, is not only physical. We also experience pollution of the soul. Call it stress, anxiety, psychic abuse, or a hundred other names, the deep structure of our soul is in disrepair. The *logos* (deep structure) of *psyche* (soul) is pretty messed up, and to date psychology has not been of notable assistance. No blame to my therapist friends, there just seems to be a little too much to do.

Nevertheless, and in spite of every prediction of immediate disaster, we continue muddling through. Something seems to be working. I submit, however, that what is working looks much more like Open Space than like the way things are "supposed" to be done. Fortunately, there is an enormous disparity between what we say and what we do. We say: "Somebody is in charge (or should be) and the system is tightly controlled." What we do is rather different. Three curious phenomena, small in themselves, suggest the nature of the difference.

First, there is the way we handle organizational charts. As a consultant, I am constantly wandering in and out of different operations. Upon arrival, the local organizational chart will be produced as a way of orienting me to the landscape, immediately followed by disclaimers about the accuracy thereof. What should be the mother lode of control and closed systems, the synopsis of "the book" by which everything gets done, turns out to be a piece of paper with little, if any, relationship to how things really happen.

Should one pursue the disclaimers and ask how it is that things *do* get done, the answer normally bears little relation to the book. Indeed, the book seems to have been lost, and getting along in its absence is a mark of experience. The difference between an experienced employee (known as an "old hand") and a newcomer (aka "greenhorn") is the ability to get along without the book. The old hand knows that nothing of importance gets done that way anyhow, while the greenhorn is still desperately searching for the lost volume.

This brings us to the second curious phenomenon. Despite all the reverence for the book and the rules of operation, it is common knowledge that following the rules will bring everything to a gooey halt, as demonstrated from time to time when those on the unionized side of the house "work to rule."

The third and last curiosity is the "work-around." Management would have you believe that there is a procedure for every necessary activity, and of course work must be done according to that procedure. But the reality is rather different. More than occasionally it is necessary to "work around" the procedures to get something done. Work–arounds are treated as exceptions, but I strongly suspect work-arounds are the rule. At least that is true with anything involving more than a modicum of challenge and/or creativity.

So things are not as they seem, which in my view suggests that circumstances are better than they appear. To some extent, this is simply a mind game, or the old optimist/pessimist routine. If we look at what *is working* in our organizations, it may turn out that the glass is half full, or better. Prospering in some reasonable style would then be less about doing something new and different and more about *becoming better and more intentional in what we are already doing, even though we try our very best to believe that we aren't doing what we really are doing.*

Doubtless that is one of the most confused sentences I have ever written, but it seems to accurately reflect the weird doublethink, doublebind that we have gotten ourselves into. In an effort to maintain a sense of control of the sort we thought we had grown accustomed to, we engage in mental gymnastics and metaphysical rationalizations sufficient to exhaust a medieval theologian. Contemplating the number of angels dancing on the head of a pin is mere child's play in comparison.

The Lessons of Open Space

Each time I have the privilege of witnessing the opening of space in an organization, I have the distinct feeling that I am observing the potential of humankind made manifest. Despite all predictions and certainties to the contrary, common people persist in doing uncommon things. Creativity and synergy abound, self-managed work teams are the norm, leadership is an everywhere/everybody phenomenon, and what is expected to take forever occurs quickly.

Not bad preparation for the emerging world that already seems to be our home. And the best part is that real people really do something. This is not a game, not a simulation, not a practice session getting ready for the real thing. It happens, and at the end of the day business has been done.

And for those still hooked on structure and control, all is not lost. Both are still very much present in the Open Space environment, but with a difference, captured by the word *appropriate.* Structure and control emerge in the natural course of business as essential ingredients for getting the job done. But primacy goes to the people and the job to be done. Structure and control appear only "as needed," and "as appropriate." Preordained structures and controls simply do not exist, or exist at very minimal levels.

It is true that for some, Open Space appears to be out of control and without structure. More often than not, however, people with this viewpoint have only heard about Open Space and never actually had the experience. Had they been there, they would know what five hundred Presbyterians discovered as they created 164 task groups in less than an hour, self-managed this monster of complexity over a thirty-six-hour period, and emerged with 350 pages of proceedings, printed and in the hands of all participants forty-eight hours after start. It was not done by levitation.

There is an enormous amount of structure and a high level of control, but all of it is generated organically and exercised by the people themselves. In short, the structures and controls are appropriate to the task at hand, the people who do it, and the environment in which they operate.

The fundamental lesson of Open Space, however, relates to the expansion of Now and the enhancement of our ability to live fully under changed, and changing, circumstances. Actually, I think it is turning out that Now has always been expanded, and it is only our perception that is (has been) constrained. As our perception changes, so do the opportunities that confront us, but all of that can be very scary. With the demise of closed systems, however, and the realization that open systems are all we have, and all we have ever had, the conditions are established for a sense of Now with no limits.

When we operate with a closed system mentality, Now is forever limited by constraining walls. Crossing from system to system, country to country, culture to culture can be accomplished only with great difficulty.

Perceived system constraints translate to ethical constraints, and somehow it becomes wrong to enter into a different time, place, worldview—and thereby leave our own proper here and now. It was intended (by whom not specified) that we should keep our place, our time, our Now. In the paraphrased words of the poignant song from *South Pacific*, "You've got to be carefully taught," we must learn to hate and fear all those our relatives hate. Christians must hate Muslims, who must hate Hindus and so on ad nauseam. And the same might be said of our competitors: IBM must crush Microsoft, who in turn will annihilate NetScape, who will obliterate.... Our perception of Now can only extend to the next set of walls created by system constraints buttressed by moral dogma.

But if the walls are understood to be permeable, or better yet arbitrary and essentially nonexistent, we are at liberty to expand to the full extent of our potential, whatever that might mean. At this point, we encounter a problem of a different sort—pure terror.

Life without limits may be a heady concept in the abstract, but as a present reality it has its drawbacks. Real, genuine freedom is not only awesome, but awful, and productive of what I call *freedom shock*. Take down the walls and you suddenly feel very naked.

Before jumping into what appears to many as a strange new environment (as if we had a choice), a little orientation may be in order. And herein lies the special gift of Open Space: it provides a safe space in which we may learn to live fully in the expanded Now.

Chapter V

Chaos and Order

When James Gleick published *Chaos* (Viking–Penguin, 1987), a number of people, myself included, said, "Wow!" Suddenly a world that defied rational description became describable. Chaotic forces and events, which seem to lie beyond any comprehensible pattern, could be appreciated in their random multiplicity and simultaneously as part of the created order.

Gleick's narrative of the emergence of chaos theory relates closely to the work of Ilya Prigogene on dissipative structures and self–organizing systems, although curiously enough, Gleick doesn't seem to recognize the affinity. In any event, Gleick and Prigogene, representing a host of others, firmly placed the notions of chaos/complexity theory and self–organizing systems into the public domain. Subsequent efforts by Margaret Wheatley in *Leadership and the New Science* (Berrett–Koehler, 1992) and others popularized the endeavor, and suddenly the fractal magic of chaos conspiring with the existing order to create constantly evolving, open, self–organizing systems became a matter of popular discourse.

As the fascination with the interplay of chaos and order, manifest in the process of self–organization, has increased, there has emerged an interesting phenomenon. It is all about *organizing* self–organizing systems. This is a strange one, and it strikes me that something is wrong with the picture. Either there is such a thing as a self–organizing system, in which case organizing one is scarcely worth the bother, or there is no such thing, in which case no amount of effort on our part will change the situation.

I suspect that just as there is no such thing as a closed system, there is no such thing as a non–self-organizing system. All systems are open and all systems are self-organizing. We show a marked tendency to gild the lily and carry coals to Newcastle by working energetically to complexify something that works pretty well by itself.

Including "all systems" in the generalization stated above may be extreme, for obviously there are a number of human-made systems (computers and manufacturing processes to name just two) that appear anything but self-organizing. As the designers would say, "We did it." True, but it is also possible to understand that the designers themselves, along with their product, are part and parcel of a larger open system, which in turn is self-organizing. Rank sophistry and gross rationalization perhaps, but the instant it is granted that everything is interconnected, the lofty isolation of "the system organizer" is questionable.

Leaving aside the sophistry for a moment, I can say that a dozen years of experience with Open Space has given me the sneaking suspicion that when it comes to creating environments for human productivity, we may be working too hard. Many of the things we do seem to add little value, and a lot of the most functional parts seem to appear naturally. Call it open systems, self-organizing systems, or just plain luck, my experience has been that groups of people, large and small, educated and not, rich and without means, all over the world create (manifest?) appropriate organization to deal with hugely complex issues, without benefit of an extensive design process, an army of facilitators, or overt external direction. Furthermore, every attempt to "prepare" people for the experience of Open Space with additional bells and whistles, exercises, or special predetermined group processes adds little to the effectiveness of the group. Such add-ons are usually perceived as pleasant sideshows at best, or more likely, just a plain waste of time.

I must emphasize that while no special effort needs to be made to prepare participants to function in an Open Space event, there is much to be done to assist the organization in usefully assimilating the Open Space experience. Before- and aftercare for the organization and those responsible are critical. But the people themselves get along just fine. No help needed.

If it should turn out that the natural laboratory of Open Space is in fact an organizational microcosm, then the possibility of scaling up to a full-size, real-time "Open Space" organization exists. It is a jump to be sure, but why not? Why can't we enjoy the pleasures of Open Space 365 days a year? I dare to believe that we can, and that Open Space experienced in a three-day event is just the appetizer, the foretaste of a marvelous banquet. The early reports (Wesley Urban Ministry, among others) suggest that possibility could become reality, but only time and careful effort (with no guarantees) can bring us to that delightful place.

So what is really going on with Open Space? Are we actually experiencing that marvelous thing called a self-organizing system? Could this be the leading edge of organization for the next millennium?

That Open Space can and does produce more productive meetings is a matter of global experience. But stopping with that experience is to miss, I think, the real significance. There is the possibility of leveraging that experience in order to achieve new, powerful ways of being in organization. Clearly we have not arrived, but the possibilities are more than intriguing. Open Space is action research at its best. In real time, we are given the opportunity to experience ourselves as we may become . . . and learn to do it all better.

The Design Principle for Open Space—Occam's Razor

Having just said that Open Space works like a self-organizing system, talking about a design principle will seem a little contradictory. Yet in the discovery process, there has been such a principle, which may be stated, *Less is more.*

For the academically inclined, I must own my debt to the medieval law of parsimony, otherwise known as Occam's Razor. Occam proposed to shave off from the theology of his day all but the essentials. Unfortunately, many of his colleagues failed to heed his advice, leading to theological embellishment beyond belief.

Open Space is minimalism with a vengeance, and means concretely that nothing but the essentials need be included. It also turns out that anything done to, or for, the people participating in Open Space detracts from what the people must do for themselves. In contemporary terms, this means disempowerment. For Open Space to "work," the power of the people must be maximized, for they alone can perceive their passions (issues, concerns) and take responsibility. Absent passion and responsibility, everything shuts down, as I learned to my sorrow on the few occasions I sought to "demonstrate" Open Space. The results were unmitigated disasters. Typically, I would pick some "made-up theme" and go through the motions. The universal response was, "Is that all there is?" No passion, no excitement, no nothing.

Operationally, the Open Space design principle comes through in the following dictum, *Think of one more thing not to do.* Each time I had the opportunity to create a little space or watch somebody else create some space, I attempted to identify one more thing, done by the facilitator during the introduction or during the course of the event, that could be eliminated. We are now down to the bare bones, and the skinnier it gets, the better it runs.

Specifically, the time necessary for the group to get itself organized and off to work has shrunk from two and one-half hours with eighty-five people to about one and one-quarter hours with seven hundred people. As an example of something I no longer do, I used to explain to people, just prior to their going to the wall en masse to sign up for the groups they wished to attend, that in the event of need, I would be around. Eventually it dawned on me that few people heard me and nobody cared. The people were already so deeply involved in what they had created that I was quite literally talking to myself.

And that, I think, is the point. Additional things to be done prior to, or during, Open Space tend to be more for the peace of mind of the facilitator (or the sponsor) than for the benefit of the people actually involved. It is my current practice, once people have gone to the wall, to leave without a word and take a walk, or more often than not, take a nap.

Working in the Domain of Spirit— Doing Nothing with Elegance

In comparison with any other facilitated group process that I am aware of, the facilitator in Open Space is apparently on extended holiday. At the conclusion of a large Open Space event, it is not uncommon for participants to come up to me with a quizzical look and words such as, "You look familiar, don't I know you from some-where?" Clearly my role as facilitator does not place me in a center stage position; this raises the reasonable question, what on earth do I do? My honest response: as little as possible. Or if that seems too flip, I indicate that I practice doing nothing with elegance, which may be even worse.

Truthfully, Open Space, from the point of view of the facilitator, is more about *being* than *doing*, and such things as are done take place on a rather different level, or in a different domain, than might be the case in more traditional approaches. The domain of Open Space is the domain of Spirit.

Talking about the domain of Spirit and what takes place there is difficult in Western culture, because little time has been spent sym-pathetically attempting to understand what might be going on there. When the domain of Spirit impinges inescapably on our lives, the normal response is to rationalize the unwanted presence in some more familiar terms, which are usually "objective" and mechanistic. Until fairly recently, standard Western practice was to assume that if you could not touch it, smell it, count it, and put it in some sort of a box, "it" did not exist.

This generalization is false, as are all generalizations, but still it would not be stretching the point to note that an outbreak of Spirit is often understood to be a mental health hazard requiring treatment. How and why we got to this place is a matter of continuing discus-sion, but the net effect has been to render many people mere babes in the woods when it comes to dealing with matters of Spirit. Even those who profess some knowledge and acquaintance are often very uncomfortable when seeking to relate Spirit to the everyday world of business, government, or communities.

Open Space, for better or worse, functions fundamentally in the domain of Spirit. Not surprisingly then, the experience appears to many as counterintuitive, strange, even downright weird, as would be the case in any situation where the fundamental mechanisms are hidden from view. While it is true that the results of Open Space may be substantive in the extreme, vastly exceeding any reasonable expectations, how those results are achieved remains a mystery. Seen from the vantage point of the domain of Spirit, however, the results are only what one might expect.

By way of analogy from a very different realm, the fundamental mechanisms of my computer are a complete mystery to me. Thus when my machine behaves oddly, I have no clue as to why, wherefore, or what next. My super-techie friends, however, just smile and say, "Of course," and quietly work some magic.

In a similar fashion, the actions, or more accurately the non-actions, of the facilitator appear no less odd, for in fact the facilitator is playing by different rules with a nonstandard deck of cards. One might even suspect a major con game. How could it be that one person standing before a group of five hundred angry and confused people, with a few simple words and in less than fifteen minutes, enables that body of folks to organize a complex task that they will accomplish over several days with minimal direction? Worse yet, that person then has the audacity to leave the group without a word and take a nap.

Spirit Space

Working in the domain of Spirit requires some special tools and techniques. There is neither the time nor the space to provide an exhaustive list, but neither is there the necessity. The ageless wisdom of humankind on the subject has been well captured in an enormous literature available on request. But just to provide a hint of some of the elements required for working in Open Space, consider the matter of space itself and how it is handled.

Certain geometric forms seem more or less hospitable to the presence of Spirit, or if you like, spirited interchange and inspired communication, which are simply different ways of saying the same thing. If you arrange people in rows, schoolroom fashion, as is common in most meetings, the net effect is passive–aggressive behavior. It is difficult, if not impossible, to genuinely communicate with the back of somebody's head. The power situation is clear. The person, or persons, at the front are in charge. They are the font of all knowledge, and the rest of the people are expected to sit down, shut up, and take notes. Presumably there are situations requiring this draconian approach, but genuine communication, in the sense of dialogue and interchange, will be rare. It is a real Spirit killer.

Should you change the geometry from rows to squares or rectangles, the stage will be set for negotiation. An immediate and predetermined hierarchy is apparent, for somebody will sit at the head (of the table), and the sides are clearly drawn. Instantaneously there is a *we* and a *they*, *us* and *them*. At the very least, this is a separated Spirit; the geometry presumes, and I rather think encourages, conflict. The individual at the head of the table is expected to keep order, or as we often say, "control the meeting." Our side of the table is placed in direct opposition to their side of the table. In a word, we have taken sides. Obviously there are practical reasons for placing people at tables, particularly if there are papers to spread out, and I am sure some highly conflicting situations may require separation of the parties. But the fundamental fact remains: positioning people around a table keeps them apart. And communication, when it occurs, occurs across the table.

The geometry of Open Space is a circle. At large Open Space events, with five hundred or more people, the circle can be quite large. On such occasions, available space requires the use of several concentric circles, but even then, the experience is one of sitting face to face *with nothing in the way.*

Throughout human history, the circle has held almost mystical qualities. It is the geometry of completeness, inclusion, wholeness. Special things happen in circles, as every indigenous group knows full well. This is the shape of the tribal council in Native America, and of the indaba in southern Africa. So-called modern society also knows the magic of the circle, reflected in such phrases as *circle of friends,* or *family circle.* Indeed, it seems that everything of importance happens in a circle, just as presidents of nations consult with their circle of advisors, and being "in the loop" (circle) is infinitely more important than any title or position. Kindergarten teachers understand the nurturing power of the story-telling circle, and women around the world enjoy the intimacy and productivity of the sewing circle.

The circle takes its place in our consciousness as the symbol of life. We begin in the primal circle of the womb, leave to join the larger circle of family, which in turn forms and re-forms in the circles of peoples and nations, friends and neighbors, peers and colleagues, all engaged in the cycle (circle) of life. Life happens in a circle. Open Space happens in a circle.

Inspiriting Space

The simple act of inviting people to join the circle is powerful in and of itself. When groups convene for an Open Space gathering, particularly if the gathering is a large one, the immediate experience upon entering the room parallels something of the awed silence encountered in a great cathedral, or indeed any sacred space. Conversation hushes, and typically people will stick to the edges. Crossing the circle is done quickly, as if to avoid some unknown threat lurking in the open space. The magic appears in the conversion of that initial experience into one of genuine communication, which often reaches surprising levels of intimacy and just plain fun, no matter how serious the issues or conflicted the participants.

The beginning of this conversion is initiated with a simple act. As the facilitator, I stand at the edge of the circle and say quietly, "Welcome to Open Space." And then with a slow, measured step, I walk the inside boundaries of the circle. The words spoken are words of invitation and acknowledgment, uttered in a cadence matching my slow pace. The exact words vary from facilitator to facilitator. Men will perform differently than women, and each individual differs from all others. But no matter the words, the intent is to invite all participants to allow their eyes to trace the boundary of the entire circle, making contact with old friends and new ones who may be strangers in the moment.

With this simple action, the circle is somehow made whole. Even though no words have passed from participant to participant, a sense of connectedness, perhaps even intimacy is manifest. The gazes of participants, having crossed the circle and connected with colleagues on the other side, invest the intervening openness with meaning and expectation. What began as foreign territory, unknown and perhaps even threatening, takes on a totally new, attractive dynamic, drawing the people to the center. Focus has been established, and Now, this present moment, is seemingly all there is.

The actual time elapsed is measured in minutes, but the time and space covered somehow appear immense. With a simple act, all of the issues and concerns, similarities and differences, conflicts and points of connection of those gathered in what can only be called solemn assembly are called forth and made present. Not a single discussion has occurred; many will happen later, but in this circle the ground is prepared, the space is opened, the journey is set to begin.

Immense time and space of a different sort have also been crossed through the simple initiatory act, for bounding the circle is one of the oldest and most traditional acts of shamans from around the world. Western, rational humankind may feel profoundly uncomfortable with this knowledge, and I confess my own surprise, combined with some degree of discomfort, when I discovered that what I took to be a natural, graceful act of welcome in fact had a history that should be acknowledged. My use of the shaman's walk in Open Space is not intended to introduce esoterica or to discomfort the participants. It is used for a single, simple reason: it works.

The species wisdom and experience carried by the shaman, combined with the primal geometry of the circle, create the initial conditions under which extraordinary human performance becomes almost commonplace and expected. Complex gatherings, which involve conflicting concerns held by diverse people, are organized in a fraction of the normal time. Design times for complex projects are reduced from an anticipated ten months to a matter of days. As Russ Natoce of AT&T remarked at the conclusion of his effort to reshape the corporate Olympic pavilion, "It's almost magic." Not really, but when one seeks to shed light on the gnawing question, what is really going on in Open Space? the answers come from some rather different, and perhaps surprising, places.

Before moving on, I feel compelled to acknowledge the obvious. I write from my own experience, my own point of view. Not every facilitator of Open Space will perform as I do nor interpret their experience as I have. But I believe one thing is held in common by all of us who have chosen to work in this area: an awareness that in Open Space we profoundly connect with the human Spirit. This awareness is at once humbling and productive of respect. It becomes clear that the minutia of the process are not the issue; personal integrity is. Further, the role of facilitator is not something to be held in perpetuity, rather it must be given away. And in fact, the dance of Open Space is one in which all participants have the opportunity, and usually the experience, of being facilitator, each for the others. There is power in the role, both in the beginning and throughout the process, but it is power that carries the responsibility to give it all away.

Chapter VI

Giving the Power Away:
The Hero/Heroine's Journey

Joseph Campbell, mythologist par excellence, has taken many people on an amazing journey. Whether one joined that journey through Bill Moyers' interviews or through the writing of Campbell himself, the trip has been an eventful one. Well past the signposts of everyday life, down into the interior reaches of humankind's soul, he has led us to the story of our genesis and growth, the mythology by which the species recorded our enlarging consciousness of self and of the possibilities for humanity.

There is much in our contemporary world that rebels at the whole notion of mythology. We know, as only endless instruction can teach, that mythology is untrue, a mere story, and our rational minds are beyond stories. We want the facts, nothing but the facts. Or so we say.

And yet when the story is told, when the mythmaker weaves and unfolds the fabric that gives our lives meaning, uncomfortable flashes of recognition break through the rational exterior. As Yogi Berra would say, "It's déjà vu all over again." We've been there, done that.

Nowhere is this sense of déjà vu more profoundly experienced than in the presence of what Campbell calls *The Hero with a Thousand Faces*, the title of his groundbreaking book (Princeton, 1949). From the dawn of history, captured by the oral traditions of early peoples, up until the present moment, heroes and heroines appear in our midst. Although the details will vary widely, the core story changes little.

Once upon a time, or even just yesterday morning, some common person did a very uncommon thing. Out of the ordinariness of everyday living a journey begins, forsaking the safety of the known for the uncharted mysteries. Threats are encountered, chaos experienced, terror and the stink of death cut to the very quick of the commoner's soul. As in the fiery alchemist's crucible, the dross is burned away, the soul is purified, and in the midst of chaos, life is reaffirmed and renewed. A hero or heroine is born.

But the story is not over. Should the new-made hero/heroine claim the powers of that new life as their personal just deserts, the heroic destiny will not be fulfilled. Here is the hardest part, a greater threat than any previous challenge: the temptation of personal glory. To claim the life-power is to lose it, for it is only in giving the gift to those who are powerless that the heroic destiny is complete. In the paradox of sacrifice, heroic meaning is made manifest. Power is powerful only when it is given away.

Open Space as the Hero/Heroine's Journey

Open Space begins in a circle, which is perceived by the participants as strange at a minimum and more usually as awesome and threatening. The facilitator begins the journey by following the path of the shaman, by bounding the circle, defining the limits, initiating the process of making the space safe, and inviting the Spirit of the people to fill the circle. When the facilitator returns to the place of starting, the role changes; shaman transmutes to hero/heroine, and a journey of a different sort begins.

The facilitator moves with determination to the center of the circle, entering deeply into territory unknown and perceived as threatening by those sitting in the circle. From a place where no person would willingly go, the assembled people are addressed: first, in terms of the reason for meeting (the theme), and subsequently to explain the four principles and the one law applicable to behavior in this new environment.

But the meaning of the words is only a small fraction of what is communicated. There is a distinct shift in the facilitator's energy and appearance. Instead of the slow, measured pacing apparent in the initial walk around the circle, the steps now become quicker, more intense, more purposeful. If the opening moments were dominated by female energy, now, as the elements of the task before the group are laid out and the principles that guide behavior are enunciated, masculine energy takes center stage.

As the words are spoken, the facilitator moves in an almost random pattern, crossing, recrossing, and crisscrossing the circle. Sometimes words are spoken in transit, and then in a moment of pause, individual participants are closely engaged and addressed. From side to side, end to end, participant to participant, invisible paths are laid, weaving a network of safety across the Open Space.

At the end, the facilitator once more stands in the center of the circle. The energy changes from purposeful search into restful mode, and words of invitation are spoken, not as a command but as a welcome. "I now invite each and every one of you who cares to, to come to the center of the circle and declare that which has heart and meaning for you. Take a piece of paper, write down your issue, sign your name, and announce both to the group. . . ."

Silence. It seems to go on forever, but measured by the clock, it is only a matter of seconds. In that silence, anxiety and expectation conflict until at last expectation triumphs. A first person stands to make the journey, followed almost instantly by many more. Suddenly the circle is filled with people hastily writing down the issue of concern for which they will take responsibility. The noise level builds as folks announce their issue and go to the wall to post it. The barren wall transforms into a public bulletin board filled with the hopes, expectations, and dreams of those present. It remains only to sign up and get to work.

And the facilitator? The role transforms again—from central focal point, to bystander, to virtual invisibility. When the people turn to the wall to make their selections and negotiate the finer points of their work together, the facilitator is left alone and unnoticed. It is time to leave.

The people now take over, and the hero/heroine's journey now becomes everyone's journey, as the mantle is transferred. Some wear the mantle well, and on others it does not fit, but each person who answers the invitation to explore an issue becomes in principle the hero/heroine in their own journey. As they convene their sessions around issues of passionate concern, they too enter into the unknown. Should they attempt the role of all-knowing leader, instructing the other participants in the truth, the Law of Two Feet almost inevitably takes over and the group will disband. But the group can, and most often does, come alive as power is distributed and given away. The hero/heroine's mantle is transferred again, and again, and again. . . .

The total time, from start until the entire undertaking has been organized with the first groups ready to go to work, is rarely more than one and one-quarter hours. Curiously, the time required for groups of 25, 250, 500 or more is identical. Of that time, a mere fifteen minutes is used by the original facilitator to establish the conditions that will take the entire group from the edge of chaos into productive activity.

In the moment, it seems like time has been suspended, or goes on forever, take your pick. This is particularly true of the awesome period lasting from the instant the invitation is issued to the participants until the first person stands to claim the center of the circle. For the sponsors of the event, particularly if they have not had previous experience with Open Space, the anxiety can become pretty intense. Will the people come? Will it work? The clock seems to go in reverse.

For myself, the moment is a wonderful combination of juicy and sacred. It is the instant of creation, and I feel privileged to be a witness. Somewhere in that silence, creativity is gestating, and while part of me is expectantly waiting for people to get on with the business, another, perhaps more substantial part, simply savors the wonder of it all.

Operating at a Deeper Level

At this juncture you may suspect an overactive imagination on my part, and perhaps the reference to the hero/heroine's journey in the context of Open Space should be taken only as a metaphor. It is certainly that, but metaphor may mutate to reality and therein lies the power of the moment.

Somehow, someway, a collective experience of the transformation of space from threatening to sacred and safe takes place within an incredibly short period of time. In fifteen minutes or less, people confronting what appears to many as an insurmountable task find themselves intimately involved in productive activity.

Explanation for this phenomenon may be impossible, or it simply may be that the commencement of an Open Space event connects participants with the deep moments of human experience alluded to in the shaman's act and the hero/heroine's journey. Whether madness, metaphor, or more, the global experience is that people move with great ease and speed. They know all the rules, indicating that perhaps they have been "there" before, which suggests, and from my point of view confirms, that what transpires in an Open Space event takes place at a rather fundamental level of human experience.

If you will grant, for the sake of argument, that the situation is as I describe it, let me say again that the development of Open Space, relative to its mythic and shamanic roots, was by no means a conscious one. Never did I or anybody else so far as I know say, "Let's take two parts shamanism, one part hero/heroine's journey, stir well, and serve when ready." The experience was always a journey of discovery. We did Open Space originally for the reasons described, seeking to avoid the frustration of discovering that the favored parts of a symposium were the coffee breaks, which basically just happened by themselves. Once on the loose, Open Space surprised everybody, and most especially me, with this curious fact: it worked. Ever since, the mystery has deepened, and we (I) have been left with the interesting questions of what works and how does it happen. The introduction of shamanism and primal mythology into the Open Space conversation simply represents two ways of dealing with those questions.

Do You Really Have to Talk Weird?

Doubtless there are many circles and places, particularly in the corporate environment, where shamanism and mythology find little if any acceptance and sympathy. If used at all, the terms become epithets of derision, pejorative and demeaning in their effect. Frankly, I often wish that I could find a more acceptable, less inflammatory way of describing what appears to be going on. It would be a supreme pity if people who needed the power and capacities made manifest in Open Space were denied access simply because the language was a little too strange.

Alternative language may exist. Yet in my experience, that language tends to be objective, rationalistic, mechanistic—in short, the language of control. And control, at least in its autocratic forms, is the nemesis of Open Space. Thus the alternatives are not real ones. Were Open Space to be reduced to the linear practicalities of a four-step method, the sense of wonder and sacredness would simply disappear. Hence, there may be some method in my madness.

I see a profound connection between the Open Space experience and the mythic realms of the shaman. Acknowledging that connection directly and without apology is, in my view, an essential "ticket of admission" to a level of reality, theory, and practice that refuses to play by the rules most of us have been taught and take for granted.

In the final analysis, words must be appropriate to the occasion of their use. Although this may make some people uncomfortable, particularly when the words appear a little "far out," the situation is not without precedent. After all, theoretical physicists have been rhapsodizing for years about the flavors of quarks, all in the name of science. It seems to come with the territory.

Personal Preparation for Facilitation

It is a joke among some of us who facilitate Open Space that we really have the best of all possible worlds. We do virtually nothing, and the client writes the report. That is just a joke, but not without an element of truth.

Under the heading of *doing*, the facilitator performs two essential functions in Open Space: creating space and holding space. The creation of space is what takes place during the first hour of the event, which has been described as the shamanic walk and the hero/heroine's journey. The business of holding space is what takes place during the balance of the time, and as an activity, it is even less demanding.

To hold space well the facilitator is required to do virtually nothing. By his or her presence, the facilitator creates the conditions of safety that allow the participants to do what needs to be done. This sounds very simple, and in a way it is. It is also highly demanding. The essential requirement is a high level of awareness that the group, in its infinite wisdom, will solve its own problems—that nothing taking place under the headings of conflict, confrontation, or some other form of altercation requires "fixing." It will all work for the benefit of the group and its purpose.

Performing in the role of facilitator can be very nervous making. First of all, the responsibilities apparently fly in the face of much of what we have been taught about enabling group process. We are supposed to have a carefully prepared agenda—wrong. We are supposed to intervene at the first sign of malfunction or discomfort—wrong. We are supposed to possess the necessary detailed knowledge to bring the group to a successful completion of its task—not only wrong but impossible.

So what are we supposed to do? Two things: *be there* and *let go*.

Being there sounds rather like "hanging out," and on the surface that is what it may look like, but in this case, as in many others, appearances can be deceiving. Being there is all about focus, presence, and clarity. We all know those times when we might "be here, but are not all there." Being there is just the opposite; it constitutes full, intentional awareness, uncluttered by all the "must–dos," side agendas, distractions, and worries of everyday life.

Operating from this state of awareness is critical to the success of any Open Space event. The reason becomes crystal clear if you simply imagine yourself entering a circle of five hundred cantankerous folks, with the task of bringing them to a point of productive activity in fifteen minutes. Any distraction will be hazardous to their mission and your mental health.

Letting go is the second critical "activity" of the facilitator. Without question, this is the hardest part. When the sessions become hot and fully engaged, there is a natural tendency to feel that we have both the skills and the duty to "make things come out right." Doing less or doing different is somehow repugnant. And yet, for Open Space to be fully open, we must get out of the way. What may appear to be an act of irresponsibility is in fact the only way to proceed if the full potential of Open Space is to be realized.

Experience to date indicates that groups will never go further into unknown territory than they can handle, even though individuals in that group may be terrified every step of the way. That "unknown" territory may be new knowledge, new relationships, or old experience now seen in a different light. In the moment it seems like a modern version of *The Perils of Pauline*, with disaster around every corner, and indeed there may be. But the presence of crisis is also the leading edge of breakthrough. The facilitator's job of watching groups navigate the thin edge separating creation and catastrophe is productive of awe, and no small amount of anxiety.

The demands placed upon anyone presuming to facilitate Open Space *on a continuing basis* are extraordinary. Not only are these demands vastly different than we might expect, they are rigorous to a fault. Having said that, and in apparent contradiction to it, I must also say that anybody with a good head and a good heart can "do" Open Space.

Paradox or contradiction, experience tells us that a onetime effort can be made by just about anybody willing to take the leap. The process is forgiving and undoubtedly will "work." If Open Space becomes something of a repeat performance, however, careful preparation is essential.

In South Africa, an individual who attended an Open Space in one of the townships walked out of our gathering and on to one of his own. Scarcely three hours after leaving our meeting he was confronting two hundred angry yet strangely apathetic folks concerned with the education of their children. Feeling that he had nothing to lose, having previously tried everything he knew to try, he went for a little Open Space. I don't know the details, but I will never forget his excited report at six o'clock the next morning. My dreams were shattered by the ring of the telephone and his insistent cry, "It worked! It worked! It worked!" When I had the wit to do so, I asked him to slow down, tell me who he was, and what had worked. He was talking about Open Space, of course, and this person's experience is not unique. But I think the rule still applies. When Open Space is the only perceived option, go for it. But if it starts to become a habit, a little training is in order.

The central problem with a repeat performance is this: having done it once, there is a natural presumption that you *know* what to do. This presumption will trip you up every single time. Knowing what to do implies that there is a right way to do it, and suddenly the old ego is involved. *Being there* becomes difficult, and *letting go* virtually impossible. At that moment, warning bells should go off in your head. While it is quite likely that the group will survive, the same may not be said for the facilitator. Open Space produces an intensity of experience that can literally blow your mind and fry your soul, if you make the mistake of presuming to control it.

There is an additional issue that makes preparation and training very useful, namely, what you do after Open Space. By now you probably understand that from my point of view, Open Space is only marginally about having better meetings. It surely will do that, but that is just the tip of the iceberg. The real payoff comes when it is possible to leverage a onetime experience into sustainable high levels of organizational performance. In sum, please try a little Open Space, but then be prepared to learn more.

Preparation for Open Space is not fundamentally about learning your lines and the steps of the process. That part is simple. Preparation is about achieving the highest level of clarity, focus, and presence that you can. There are doubtless a million ways to do this, and no one way is right for all people. For myself, I find that several hours of deep meditation works well. If an event is to start at nine o'clock in the morning, you will find me hard at work, so to speak, no later than five o'clock that morning. By the time I step into that circle, I am as ready as I will ever be.

Over the years, I have come to a core insight: Open Space begins with me—or with whoever is the facilitator. To be effective, "ownership of the space" must quickly pass to the total group, but at the moment of initiation, the facilitator holds it all. This fact carries an enormous responsibility. At some level the people assembled have placed their lives in my hands, sometimes quite literally. It is incumbent upon me to serve them, and to quickly return that which was theirs from the beginning, the space in which to accomplish their task. Being ready to assume this responsibility is what preparation is all about.

It starts with a very small Now as my eyes struggle to open in the predawn darkness. Given what I do, there are times when I am lucky to know what city I am in, let alone the correct time. When you are foggy about time and space, being fully present is difficult.

Starting from this less than inspiring point, it is essential that I not only achieve a degree of waking consciousness, but most importantly, broaden that consciousness to include, or at least be open to, the full dimensions of the people and purpose with whom I will be working. This is not about knowing all the details, for I don't and couldn't. It is about preparing an expectant place for them in my heart, with plenty of room and a challenge to grow.

Once under way, preparation turns to preservation, the business of keeping yourself in serviceable condition during the course of the event. No small amount of preservation is physical, and it is here that my nap becomes critical. If I am up and about in the early morning hours, and then engage in a brief, but energy intensive, opening session, by the time that session is concluded, I am whipped. Presuming I want to be functioning well for the balance of the affair, I need to take care of myself right then and there.

Preservation has other dimensions as well. Keeping in mind that the observable interventions of the facilitator during the course of an event are minimal to nonexistent, it is reasonable to ask what I am doing. My activities are generally limited to picking up coffee cups and trash, and on occasion arranging chairs. I may also be seen sitting amid the computers, assisting with the preparation of the proceedings. And yet my presence is integral to the whole process, at least that is what the participants tell me, which corresponds with my own feelings. So what am I doing? My answer is holding space for the Now to grow in, or creating the safe environment in which the people's potential may be fully present, Now. Same thing said in a different way.

My role is not to "do" anything. Doing is the job of the participants. But in order for them to do their work, they need safe space. Maintaining (holding) that safe space is my job. As a job description, this may leave something to be desired, and for a facilitator, part of the challenge of Open Space is coming to a fuller understanding of just what is transpiring. But seen from the inside, and therefore completely subjectively, the job "looks like" 99 percent intuition and 1 percent overt activity.

In order to be with the participants wherever they happen to be and whatever they happen to be doing, lending encouragement and support, my intuition has to be turned up to high range and any "stuff" that could get in the way must be removed. That includes, for example, my expectations for specific outcomes, any judgment on my part as to the adequacy of performance by the participants, and physical distractions such as hunger and fatigue. Maintaining this high-level alert cannot be done without intention and effort, which is what I mean by preservation.

Is There Something More Here?

I can appreciate that for some people my description of the facilitator's role and preparation passes beyond reasonable comfort zones. Open Space is not for everybody. But I can report that working in

Open Space has become infinitely more than a role or a job; it has become a way of life, one which I find enjoyable and fulfilling.

At the simplest level, life in Open Space is economical in the extreme, devoid of wasted energy and useless frills. At the end of an intense and productive event, or even a succession of them, I find myself tired but by no means exhausted or drained. Often I experience a wonderful, rosy glow derived from a profound sense of accomplishment, which is largely not mine. I find it possible to move with ease from one complex and conflicted situation to another, each situation providing its own pleasure as common people do uncommon things with regularity. It is my privilege to witness fellow human beings engage the vicissitudes of the moment with style and competence. Life could definitely be worse.

More profoundly, I am coming to the conclusion that what I have experienced episodically with each discrete Open Space event can, in fact, be descriptive, or better yet prescriptive, of enhanced organizational function. It doesn't take a wizard to tell us that the rate and degree of transformation currently experienced at all levels in our global society will only increase. Nor do we need that wizard to inform us that the current way we have chosen to cope with the ongoing transformation leads to stress, burnout, personal abuse, and other soul-destroying results.

We can, of course, simply abdicate the field. Some of us have done this, and all of us are tempted. If, however, there were a way not only to rise to the challenge but also to actually enjoy the enterprise, wouldn't that be grand? I think there is such a way, or at least that has been my experience.

Chapter VII

What Next?

*I*t is my fondest hope that by 2010 (just to pick a date), Open Space, as a distinct methodology, will have disappeared from the face of the earth. It is not that I wish to rid the earth of Open Space, I simply hope that the methodology will have become so commonplace as to be invisible. I envision Open Space to be rather like accounting— something everybody does—noticed only when it is not done or done poorly.

This hope for the invisibility of Open Space Technology is not without foundation. If you will grant my strong suspicion that a majority of the truly workable aspects of our present organizations look much more like Open Space than the standard picture of command and control, we are already well on the way. Add the notion that the current high-stakes environment has created conditions fostering organizational evolution in the direction of Open Space, and 2010 may well be further into the future than Open Space Technology will extend.

No claim is made for the evolutionary cards being stacked in favor of Open Space, or alternatively, for having designed Open Space to fit current evolutionary trends. But I do not think it takes extreme perception to understand that organizations surviving with style in the next millennium will be flexible, fun, and hugely efficient in terms of human energy and Spirit—always enlarging their awareness of an enormously dynamic world—in short, living very intentionally in an expanding Now. The alternative is virtually instantaneous burnout, isolation, and obsolescence, none of which are particularly good for business. Open Space may be able to help in several areas.

A New Mental Model

In the language of the moment, I venture to predict that Open Space will effectively become the mental model for life in organizations. The achievement of this position will not take place because of argument, coercion, or command. Indeed, the use of any of these would violate the core principle of Open Space and send the organization in precisely the opposite direction. In a word, executive dictate is nonoperative when it comes to following the Open Space path.

But how, you might ask, will this miracle occur? Absent proclamation by the CEO, can anything possibly take place? Certainly, and for two very simple reasons: Open Space works and Open Space feels good.

The new mental model, based upon Open Space, will have a number of dimensions. First and most obvious will be an alternative geometry for the organizational image. In place of the present ranked silos or stepped hierarchy, there will be a circle. The language will change from the upstairs/downstairs motif, as in "I'll take that idea upstairs for approval," to words like *across, together, collaborate*. To the extent that perception is reality, decision making and its corollaries will no longer be seen as happening far away, but rather in the immediate environs. Practically, this should mean smoother, faster operations, particularly on those days when we feel too tired to go all the way upstairs.

Secondly, there will be an elevated notion of expected human performance. In effect, the bar will have been raised. Self-managed work groups, distributed leadership, and the enjoyment of work will no longer be way out there in the future, to be experienced only after we have completed all the training programs and reorganized for the final time. Such things will have been done, and we will go from there.

Thirdly, and from my point of view most profoundly, the perceived essence of organization will have expanded from the present fixation on the bits and pieces, plant and facility, bottom line and quarterly results, to include the full realm of the human Spirit. Such things as intuition, expanded consciousness—even love—will be seen as critical to organizational function. Of course the bits and pieces, and particularly the bottom line, will still be important, but no longer the only thing.

New Paths for Assessment and Compensation

Assume for a moment that organizations in the next millennium will look rather like an Open Space event. Leadership pops up where it is needed and as it is needed. Work groups form, reform, and disappear. Diligent search for *the leader* comes up empty-handed, and management, as an exclusive command and control function exercised by a special class of people, is absent from view.

This may be a strange new world from many perspectives, but it is virtually incomprehensible from the viewpoint of current assessment and compensation practices. Check any employee evaluation form for the critical elements of assessment. Ordinarily they are: How many people do you supervise? Have you managed to keep them under control, and if so, for how long? Lastly, do you actually know what you are doing (as in possess some defined body of knowledge)?

High scores along these several parameters justify an elevated position in the organization and more money in the paycheck. With minor modifications, this is the way we have been doing business for years, and at the end of the day it appears fair, orderly, and effective.

The nicely ordered world of assessment and compensation, however, quickly falls apart in Open Space. After all, nobody is in charge as a matter of preexisting right; individuals may simultaneously be members and leaders of several different task groups, all of which may change in a moment. Bodies of knowledge seem to come and go with abandon, and what was hot stuff this afternoon is cold porridge by tomorrow morning. Given all of the above, how do you fairly compensate individuals, and can you even think of assigning them to fixed positions with predetermined authority and responsibility? If the answer is clearly no, the solution to the dilemma is less apparent.

There are some clues, however. If one were to consider the world of consultants as a business, not just *individuals in business,* it is arguable that this world runs by the rules of Open Space. Nobody is in charge, people follow what has "heart and meaning" for them, even if that boils down to what the client will pay for, and the Law of Two Feet always applies. If you don't like the heat in the kitchen, you know where the door is.

Some people may view the consultant's world as a primitive jungle, but as an inhabitant, I find it quite ordered and very much to my liking. Generally speaking, quality rises to the top—not always and not instantaneously—but sooner or later incompetence is not rewarded and questionable ethics are punished by neglect of the practitioner. In this kind of environment, position is almost inevitably a function of peer acknowledgment, and compensation a function of what the market will allow.

There is a kind of frontier justice that works more often than not, and perhaps with some refinement it might actually serve as a model. Doubtless, rough edges need smoothing, but I submit we are not without recourse when it comes to possible alternatives to the current compensation system.

New Paths for Training and Development

If assessment and compensation are thrown into something of a tail–spin by Open Space, the impact on training and development is infinitely more profound. Recall the remarks of the American Society for Training and Development (ASTD) executive. (See page 4.) I am quite positive that his estimate of 95 percent redundancy is a trifle high, but there is little question that much that is currently done under the heading of training and development, in terms of either content or approach, would not be necessary in an Open Space organization.

It is already becoming apparent to many line managers/senior executives that significant portions of training, as it is currently done, represent an expensive luxury that is increasingly hard to justify in a cost–cutting environment. Leave the money aside, and justification is still difficult. Sooner or later it has to be recognized that for all the time and effort expended on such things as leadership, empowerment, self–managed work teams, diversity, learning organizations, and the like, the actual return on investment is questionable. Each of these has come (and sometimes gone) in the mode of fad–of–the–week. Rather like the quality circles of several years back, they pop up like mushrooms in the night and may be on the way to disappearing without a trace.

Enhanced technical skills will always be required, and the training necessary to produce them is essential. Where I think we are in trouble is on the "soft side" of the street. Whether you call these skills "people skills" or something else, a consensus seems to be growing that the goods have not been delivered. Clearly this is not due to lack of effort, for many good, bright people have devoted their lives to the undertaking. And I would be in gross error to paint a picture of total failure, but even the most optimistic will probably have to admit that the promises made have not always been promises kept.

The *why* in this situation is an interesting question that might be addressed in terms of system constraints militating against distributed leadership, real empowerment, and the like. You can train people any way you want, but when they are placed back into a system that will not tolerate the very thing they are trained for, the net result can only be nil or worse. The *worse* consisting of being told one thing offsite and having to confront the diametric opposite back on the job come Monday morning.

Frankly, it is enough to make true believers despair, and some have already done so. The problem is: it is precisely these "soft people-skills" that make all the rest work. Technical competence without the ability to collaborate is not a prescription for staying in business.

In Open Space, and in the small number of organizations consciously running in Open Space, some rather different things take place. Distributed leadership, self-managed work teams, celebration of diversity, meaningful community, all appear on cue as a natural part of the order of things, suggesting that they were already present, obscured only by our attempt to keep everything under control.

When capacities are already present, it makes little sense to train for their arrival. It makes a lot of sense to build on what already exists. Thus, in the presence of distributed leadership, one might ask how to make it deeper, more powerful, more shared. Or given self-managed work groups, how does one acknowledge that reality and build superior self-managed work groups?

If Open Space does nothing else in terms of organizational function, it benchmarks that function at a new and higher level. Organizations that consciously operate in Open Space will *start* at the new benchmark and go up from there. The function of training and development will be to assist in the process, and there is clearly an awful lot of work to be done. But it won't necessarily be what we are doing now.

Perhaps the most innovative and exciting area for training and development to explore will be the so-called *subtle realms.* I truly hesitate to mention this, as it will make some people quite uncomfortable and convince others that the total effort represented here is nothing short of witchcraft. But moving right along and throwing caution to the wind—just imagine future programs on *The Shamanic Way* paired with *Contemporary Mythmaking.* The mind boggles, but the possibilities are intriguing.

New Paths for the Body Politic

One of the universal signs of the times is political gridlock and governmental malfunction. All over the world and with infinite variation, the tried and true political systems on the planet lie in disrepair. Currently, Italy is on its fifty-fifth government since the end of World War II; Canada is engaged in intense debate about the nature, and even the continuance, of its national union; and of course, here in the United States, we have an ongoing standoff between Congress and the White House.

Many people despair of "the system," by whatever name or national origin. The net result is apathy born of frustration, or revolution born of the same parent. We all know, however, that apathy and disengagement are nonsolutions. Blaming the politicians is scarcely any better. At some significant level, Pogo was right: *We have met the enemy, and the enemy is us.* On the political front, particularly in the democratic West, we pretty much get what we ask for, or passively allow to happen.

So where do we go from here? Some people suggest that Open Space might be a useful replacement for current political systems. After all, it seems to work, it's fun, and it's productive of concrete results. That suggestion may go a little too far, but the experience to date suggests that Open Space can make a very useful contribution to the overall political process.

In South Africa, during the intense nation–building process preceding the formal abolition of the all–white national government, the platform for negotiation was called CODESA. With the wisdom of hindsight, it appears that CODESA not only worked, but worked rather well to achieve its major goal, the bloodless transfer of power. But in the moment, virtually all observers, black or white, agreed—CODESA was definitely a white–knuckle trip. For every step forward there seemed to be five steps backward, followed by several to the side.

During one of the more confusing periods, a little Open Space was suggested for CODESA's table. There was some question as to the actual possibility of doing that, but little question that the effort *would not* have been rewarded by success. The problem had nothing to do with the capacity of Open Space to work in strange places; it can and it does. But formal political mechanisms also work, and they have an important, distinct, but limited job to do. That job is to rationalize and institutionalize the desires of the people as elaborated in prior conversations.

Political mechanisms are all about *yes* or *no, up* or *down, either/or.* They require people to take positions, and although compromise and conversation are possibilities, the possibilities are limited at best. That does not make political mechanisms bad, just limited. What is bad is when we force the political mechanism to go beyond its limitations and do what it was never designed to do—create a space for conversation.

Useful conversation is best conducted out of the spotlight and away from the hearing rooms. This is not a proposal for a return to smoke-filled rooms and secret deals, but rather a simple recognition that prior to decision making, it is useful to understand what you are deciding about and what the alternatives may be. Building that sort of understanding requires asking "dumb questions," and dumb questions are best asked in a degree of privacy.

Several years ago in Washington, D. C., when I was deeply engaged in the national health-policy arena, one of the most significant contributions to the entire enterprise came from a most unlikely source. Periodically, usually once a month, Judy Miller gave a dinner party. Each party would focus on a specific issue, such as Medicaid reimbursement. Senior government people who had a significant stake in that issue were invited, and everything was off the record. Such press as was present understood and obeyed the rules, or else. There were few if any speeches, and the bar was open for an extended period. In

the midst of it all, Judy did her thing as the gracious, informed host-
ess she was.

Result? People talked. They asked dumb questions. They cleared
up misunderstandings. They laid the groundwork for effective solu-
tions, legislative and otherwise. But mostly they talked. I can't prove
it, but I think it is fair to say that no significant piece of health-care
legislation emerged in that period that was not positively shaped by
Judy's dinner parties.

Judy's brainchild was not without precedent. The *salon* has been
part and parcel of the political/intellectual scene since either began.
An earlier form was the *agora* in ancient Athens. The agora was the
marketplace not only of goods but also of ideas. The great conversations of the day were carried out there, presumably with a little
refreshment along the way. Actually the agora was probably the
original Open Space, which we still recognize in the modern English
word *agoraphobia*, the fear of open space. Well, we need not be afraid,
but you get the idea.

Under the best of circumstances, and no matter where it starts,
good government seems to require good conversation. And there
needs to be a continuum, from conversation in relative privacy
through public discourse in the halls of government. The former is
exploratory, the latter definitive. Somehow we seem to have put the
cart before the horse, rushing to judgment over issues we don't
understand. The results are predictable and disastrous. Having asked
government to do what it never could (or should) do, we then blame
it for failing. But the failure is ours, and so is the blame. We simply
didn't do our homework.

Enter Open Space. Having read this far, you know that Open Space
is fast, cheap, and can easily handle large numbers of cantankerous

people, attributes of more than incidental utility given the present condition of the body politic. More to the point, Open Space offers a safe space within which useful conversation may take place leading to the clarification of issues and development of consensus. In short, Open Space is a good place to do our homework. The Canadians are trying all this out, and while the plan and execution may not have been perfect, the learning has been enormous. Who knows where Open Space may next break out in the body politic.

Cyberspace and Open Space

From the very first time that Open Space appeared in Monterey, California, up to the present moment, there has always been a close connection with the world of computer conferencing, which the cognoscenti have labeled cyberspace. As with most things relating to Open Space, planning was not part of the equation. It just turned out that Frank Burns and Lisa Carlson of the MetaNetwork (one of the earliest computer conferences) were participants in that first Open Space event and brought their computers along. The connection was made then, and I think it is fair to say that a substantial proportion of the conferees at that initial Open Space never appeared in physical form. Rather they manifested electronically from all over the planet.

It sounds rather weird when you say it like that, but it is the truth. From Europe, Japan, and all over North America, folks actively participated in the discussions. New ideas generated in cyberspace were posted on the (physical) conference walls, and summaries of the conference discussions were uploaded for global dissemination.

Today all of that sounds pretty "old hat," but in 1985 it was quite on the leading edge. And we learned a lot. Perhaps most surprising was the impact of the global electronic connection on the face-to-face conference. It would be no exaggeration to say that because of electronic visitors, the total conference quickly began to run on global time. There literally never was a time that something was not happening, and for that reason normal nine to five conference hours went totally out the window.

The cybernetic connection added more than a global sense of time. The gift, quite simply, was a *global sense*—period. Somehow, in a manner undefinable, we (all participants—physical and electronic) experienced a deep connection that simply obliterated the normal time/space constraints. We were one.

Our oneness was experienced not so much as a mystical relationship of some sort but rather as a very practical connection. There was an organic interrelationship that proved conducive to productive activity. In short, we got things done with dispatch and in the manner of what Peter Vaill, in *Managing as a Performing Art* (Jossey-Bass, 1989), has called a High Performing System.

The learning has continued, and if anything, is escalating exponentially. Multisite, simultaneous Open Spaces are not exactly commonplace, but they are also by no means revolutionary, which means that the total number of participants in any Open Space event is theoretically unlimited. The practical application and positive contribution to such areas as strategic planning and community project design should be obvious. Since numbers are not a problem, there is no reason to exclude anybody, leading to genuine, broad-based participation, which in turn points toward enhanced "buy-in" (ownership) and implementation.

But this, I think, is just the beginning. We already know how to bring working communities effectively online, in real time, globally. In the twinkling of an eye, time and space no longer mean what they used to. And that is just for openers. Add in some exotic software such as the neural-network wonder-worker marketed by a company called TASC under the name Information Refinery, and you really have something to conjure with.

The software behind the Information Refinery was originally designed for unmentionable government agencies analyzing electronic communications originating from the "other side." With the outbreak of peace, the prodigious capacity of this software is now available to communities and corporations alike. In a demonstration, I watched 413,000 journal and press articles being analyzed in just over a minute, with their contents mapped and cross correlated. Mindblowing. Put this together with Open Space and minds will really be blown.

Just imagine five thousand folks from Corporation *X* gathered simultaneously in ten locations around the globe for the annual strategic update. As each location identifies issues and opportunities, all locations are notified. And when the discussion from any group is entered into the computer system, it appears simultaneously everywhere. Good ideas from San Francisco show up instantaneously in London, Paris, Canberra, and Capetown.

But the fun is just beginning. When several reports have been entered, the good old Information Refinery swings into action, analyzing each report for interrelationships and common themes. The first several attempts are pretty much "garbage," but with practice, the software gets smarter. Suddenly there is a critical base: related themes from all over the world are connected and their authors informed so the synergy may expand, if that is their pleasure.

And that ain't all! With a little instruction from its handlers, the Information Refinery turns outward, seeking interesting correlations from global databases with the ongoing discussions at Corporation *X*.

A brilliant new product idea probably needs to be looked at again because according to a little-read professional journal, the underlying chemical process just happens to produce carcinogens by the carload. Somehow the engineers of Corporation *X* missed this small point. But the Information Refinery didn't.

And of course, everything is captured for future use. Names and addresses of all the participants, their discussion, even the explorations of the Information Refinery, are stored and instantly available for use and/or update.

It dawns on the five thousand participants that their exercise in strategic planning need not be an annual once-done-soon-to-be-forgotten phenomenon. Planning can become truly useful as daily support for ongoing work, for it is not locked in concrete but available for use and responsive to changing global conditions.

Without major struggle, executive intervention, or the guidance of external consultants, corporate integration at a truly significant level (let's call it wholeness, or a full sense of Now) is within reach as three essential organizational functions merge and interact. *Planning, doing,* and *learning* become a matter of emphasis and not separable functions, for any corporate act is all three simultaneously. To do is to plan is to learn—and the efficiencies achieved are staggering. Customers and stockholders are delighted with quality, price, and return on investment respectively. As for the employees, they discover the system suddenly to be their friend, supporting their work rather than acting as an obstacle to be overcome or worked around. Happiness abounds, except of course in those places and with those persons previously known as the planning or training departments. They no longer exist as separate entities now that doing, learning, and planning all fit together.

Science fiction? Of course, but the pieces are all there, and not too long into the future we'll get it all together. In the meantime, the cybernetic connection continues to grow. After all, Open Space and cyberspace seem to go together like cake and ice cream. If you doubt that just check out the Internet and experience the biggest Open Space on Earth.

Organization as Spirit: The Gift of Open Space

For all of us at sometime, and for many of us still, the essence of organization, or an organization, is understood through the "hard stuff," typically talked about as size and structure. Given information regarding how big an organization is and the way it is organized, most of us feel a degree of comfort with our knowledge about that entity. We then may spend no small amount of time and effort seeking the optimal size and structure. Currently it seems that small is in and hierarchy is out. But that could change. It has changed before.

Whereas size and structure have been seen as the elemental core of organizational life, the Open Space experience suggests that neither are all that important, and certainly they are not determinative. Thus we have the curious phenomenon that the function and feel of groups of ten or of one thousand operating in Open Space are virtually identical. It takes them roughly the same time to get organized, they do essentially the same thing, and at the end of the day, the affective conditions (how it feels) are, for all purposes, identical.

Conditions for participation in Open Space are simple in the extreme. "Whoever cares" and "as many as it takes" typically cover the necessary considerations. From there on out, size and structure vary widely and change constantly. The optimum is whatever seems to work.

So what is the core reality of an organization? I would have to say Spirit. This statement is not subject to proof and is obviously open to multiple interpretations, to say nothing of misunderstandings. But Spirit still gets my vote. The reason is basically a matter of experience.

In every Open Space event I have attended, and in all organizations where Open Space has become, to some conscious degree, an everyday experience, the environment can only be described as high-spirited. The pacing, tasks, outputs, language, culture, and business vary all over the map, but the quality of Spirit is significant by its similarity. Clear. Focused. Present. Now.

Using a word like Spirit, particularly with a capital *S*, cries out for definition. But in all honesty I can't define it, nor do I feel any necessity to do so. Spirit is one of those realities we all recognize when it is present, and conversely, are acutely aware of in its absence. When Spirit is up, marvelous things can happen. And when Spirit has gone south, no amount of money in the bank, competency in the staff, or whiz-bang technology in the back room is going to change the fact that things do not seem to be working at a fundamental level. As far as I am concerned, the essence of Spirit can remain a mystery. Indeed, it may well be that accepting mystery, and learning to live with it, constitute the first steps toward an understanding of Spirit.

There are undoubtedly many factors, theoretical and practical, that contribute to an outbreak of Spirit, but I sense that the fundamental forces are quite simple. When passion, otherwise known as Spirit, is invited to show up in a responsible way, structure and control naturally assume a supportive role. The net effect is that Spirit appears as the powerful essence and core of an organization, for nothing is getting in the way.

Far from being an esoteric, other-worldly manifestation, I find Spirit to be an in-your-face practicality. When Spirit is present, there is an ease of being, a degree of authenticity that is positively disarming and absolutely productive of extraordinary results. Life definitely could be worse, as Now expands and wholeness manifests.

Chapter VIII

Expanding Our Now:
A Journey to Wholeness

*E*xpanding our Now, my image and metaphor for Open Space, is fundamentally about reestablishing the wholeness of our lives. And at the moment, our lives, both individual and organizational, mostly seem to be falling into pieces. It would be easy to blame the traumatic events of our times for this condition, but I think those events are more symptomatic than causative. I see the piecemeal nature of our experience as coming from a different place, and as largely of our own making. In a word, I think we are shooting ourselves in the foot, a concept that contains both bad news and good news. The bad news is obvious; the good news is that we could stop, given the intention to do so.

Peter Vaill, sometime dean of the business school at George Washington University, describes the role of the professor as "making distinctions with distinction." It seems that the professors of this world have done an outstanding job, for the fabric of life has been cut into ever finer pieces. We now know more and more about less and less, and somewhere in the process, the connectedness of everything has been lost to view.

It is not fair, of course, to blame the fracturing of existence totally on the professors, but the Western infatuation with detailed knowledge of the facts, nothing but the facts, has certainly had its impact. Our way of knowing is typically the way of dissection. Thus, to know a frog is to cut it into small pieces and study each piece in detail. Only recently has it begun to dawn on us that at the end of the day we don't know the frog, just the pieces. Those pieces can be cut into smaller pieces, and so on ad infinitum.

What is true for frogs is also true for organizations and for individual lives. For the Western rational mind, organizations become comprehensible when the details are laid out, when the parts are separated. Departments, branches, centers, budget items, separable tasks, all in their distinctness, supposedly provide us with an awareness of the organizational identity.

As individuals, we become the sum total of our constituent parts: brain and liver, family and friends, jobs and hobbies. Give me the parts and I can perceive the whole.

Fixation on the parts of life, whether individual or organizational, is not totally wrong nor is it evil. Indeed, there is much power in this way of looking at things, and most if not all of what we know as modern medicine, high technology, mass production—"the good things in life"—could not have occurred without it.

Not terribly far beneath the surface of our love affair with the pieces of life, however, is the desire for control and the illusion that we actually can possess it. Practically speaking, if we have a problem area, the automatic response is to break it into its constituent parts, fix the broken part, and presumably restore normal functioning to the whole. When a business is heading south, for example, we look for the offending part—be it marketing, sales, or finance—and do a "fix." If minor surgery can do the job, so be it, otherwise transplantation is in order. Heads will roll, reorganization will eliminate inefficiency, and the well-oiled machine will be back in working order. Chaos has been averted and control restored.

As individuals, we approach life's difficulties with a similar mentality. We analyze the problem and determine the fix: adjust the ego,
replace the heart, fine-tune the hormonal system. Somewhere the
correct pill, surgical procedure, or self-development technique exists
to bring our life under control.

We are beginning to learn that things don't always work as the
Western rational mind would have them work. This is relatively new
knowledge. Until fairly recently, the problem-fixer reigned supreme,
and faith in the ultimate ability of humanity to analyze, fix, or replace
whatever seemed to be broken in the system survived without dent.
To be sure, there were a few glitches here and there, but they might
be perceived as suitable challenges for the ever-expanding human
ability to "fix" the problem. Even those of us who followed what
might be termed alternative, more holistic paths in life had the same
idea. As an early member of the U. S. Peace Corps, I and my ten
thousand colleagues were off to fix the world, secure in the certainty
that we either knew, or could identify, the broken pieces.

Planet Earth has been teaching us some valuable, albeit fairly painful lessons in recent days. These lessons are coming closer together
and cumulatively seem to be having the desired effect. The complexity and interconnectedness of life's totality swells as a tidal wave,
serving notice that the tiny island of analyzers and fixers is at some
risk. The way of rational analysis is not so much wrong as simply
inadequate to the task.

It is a little hard to say which lessons have been critical, and surely
each person will have their favorite (or unfavorite). For myself, the
gas crunch in the early 1970s hit home. Lining up at the gas station at
five o'clock in the morning made it painfully clear to me that we
were dealing with a nonrenewable resource upon which we were

overly dependent. Furthermore, we—all six billion of us resident on the planet—contributed to the situation by carrying out seemingly disrelated and possibly trivial activities, which in their total inter-action, left our minds boggling and left me sitting in the gas line. In the short term, we might find a quick fix, as in drilling another oil well, but no amount of "fixing" at that simple level was going to change the situation. Only a mind-shift would do. Now there is a "problem" worthy of the name—planetary mind-shift.

The list of wake-up calls continues. The latest tropical hurricane, the blizzard of 1996, the Mississippi River reclaiming its rightful domain despite the U. S. Corps of Engineers' efforts at "flood control" . . . all make the point. We can't even think at the level of complexity required to understand such events, let alone identify the offending pieces in order to achieve a fix. Indeed, it seems that greater sophisti-cation of tools and methods, designed for more precise appreciation of the parts and pieces, only results in an expanded realization of the infinity of possibilities. We have entered the world of *Alice in Wonder-land*, where the faster we go the behinder we get. Surely there is a better way.

The Systems Approach

In the early 1980s, Charlie Kiefer, president of Innovation Associates and close associate of Peter Senge of learning organization fame, posed an interesting question, "How do you think about wholes?" Charlie put his finger precisely on the issue we have been wrestling with here. Dealing with parts is effective in some limited situations, but parts have meaning only in terms of the whole, and how do you think about the whole? Not just think, mind you, but place oneself in a position where useful action may proceed from thought. At the time, the answer appeared to come from systems theory, the brain-child of Ludwig Bertalanffy and his colleagues.

Ludwig von Bertalanffy's *General System Theory* (Braziller, 1968) was a groundbreaking, mind-busting effort. Thanks to Peter Senge and *The Fifth Discipline* (Doubleday, 1990), the world of systems theory became infinitely more accessible to everyday organizations and businesses. The intent in both cases (Bertalanffy and Senge) was to think constructively about wholes. In a conscious effort to reverse the process of fractionalization, these gentlemen, among others, made a major effort to put the Humpty-Dumpty of our splintered world together again.

But when all is said and done, I can't help feeling that what we are left with is still parts. Albeit the parts are now connected, and the whole is understood to be more than the sum of the parts. Still, however, we have parts. As all the king's horses and all the king's men discovered, once shattered, Humpty-Dumpty is very difficult to reassemble. My learning is: to think about wholes, you have to start with wholes, in their wholeness, for the whole time. In a word, don't drop Humpty-Dumpty.

Uneasiness with the systems approach, to give it a generic title, is not mine alone. Ken Wilber, whose work I respect enormously, comes out in a similar place. In *A Brief History of Everything* (Shambala, 1996), which is actually a synopsis of Wilber's magnum opus with the even more outrageous title *Sex, Ecology and Spirituality* (Shambala, 1995), he argues that the problem with systems thinking as presently carried out is not that it is wrong, simply that it is incomplete. The systems approach does an outstanding job when it comes to objective (exterior) elements of our experience, individually and collectively. Such things as planets, nation-states, limbic systems, and brains are all treated very effectively. They are, after all, such that they may be seen, touched, tasted, or heard either directly or through some extended mechanism. They are also proper objects of rational thought, in one form or another.

Left out of the systems approach, however, is the whole world of interiorities, such as emotions, concepts, symbols, and myths, which may only be apprehended through rather different means. Of course, one is at liberty to simply discount the entire realm of interior subjectivity, which Wilber says is precisely what we in the West have done. I would agree. And the cost is considerable. We are left with what Wilber calls *monological flatland*. Even without precise definition, I am sure you can catch the flavor. This is life without meaning, for all the subjective warm fuzzies have been dropped out. Likes, dislikes, passions, and emotions are excluded. All the stuff by which we value the flavors of our lives is thrown out the window, leaving a very sterile existence. And of course, Spirit is outlawed.

Actually, as I think about it, the problem is thinking, or more exactly an exclusive dependence on thinking (thought) as the way to knowledge. The rational process and its Western practitioners do precisely what Peter Vaill said they do: make distinctions with distinction. Wholes are rationalized into their constituent elements, which in turn are further subdivided in an unending, and unendable, search for the core kernel of truth. Somewhere, under all this stuff, there must be the critical piece that makes everything work, or not work.

The Way of Contemplation

There is another way, which we might call contemplation. I am not terribly happy with this word, but I think it points in the right direction. In the West, contemplation is often viewed as soft, muddle-headed thinking that totally disregards the constituent facts by look-ing only at the whole. This charge is quite warranted if the only way to knowledge is thought, but much of the world would dispute both the charge and the *exclusive* reliance on thought as the way to truth.

Approaches to contemplation are as varied as the traditions of humankind. But all peoples seem to have discovered ways to clear their minds and hearts of disconcerting chaff and clutter in order to achieve focus, clarity, and attention. And when the whole becomes the focus of our attention, wholeness appears in clarity.

Thinking has its place, and so does contemplation. The objective of both may be similar, or the same, but the approach is diametrically opposite. Thinking thrives on bits, pieces, and facts—driving through them to the heart of the matter. Contemplation appreciates the whole in its wholeness and allows the heart to emerge, not as separable from the whole but as its essence.

In fact, a substantial portion of Peter Senge's work resides in the area of contemplation, and it may be only some of his contemporary interpreters who overlook, or fail to emphasize, this aspect. The sec-tion of *The Fifth Discipline* on personal mastery, one of the five disci-plines, makes it exquisitely clear that Senge is no stranger to the world of contemplation.

The revelation of Senge's contemplative side should come as no surprise to anyone who has participated in the Leadership and Mastery Program, which was, and probably still is, the flagship effort of Innovation Associates, with which Senge has long been identified, along with Charlie Kiefer. General systems theory and systems dynamics are made experientially present in that program through the famous "beer game." Program participants battle the vagaries of system functioning to bring the brew to thirsty customers. It is a game nobody can win; the harder one thinks and the more rational one becomes, the further away customer satisfaction appears to move.

A humbling learning takes place for all involved. You simply can't get there from here—at least by thinking about it. With despair only non-seconds away, the cavalry, in the form of a simple, contemplative approach, comes charging in. What you can't think, you can contemplate, and then you can act on that contemplation. Implicit in that action is the utilization of thought in all its forms, from program analysis to budgetary forecasting. But that is secondary. The starting point is contemplation of the whole, yielding a conscious awareness of the totality, even though the concrete details are less than clear at the start.

The Expanding Now in Open Space

The critical gift of Open Space is the experiential awareness of the whole, or in words we have used to this point, a firm foundation in Now. Now is experienced as seamless. It may be a small Now or a big Now, but it is all Now. As the perception of Now expands, the magnitude and texture of the whole is perceived. This is quite different from thinking about something, for thought drives toward pieces. There is a degree of violence present in thinking, as the whole is separated into parts and Humpty-Dumpty is disassembled.

The domain of Now, which in reality is the hometown of Spirit, is never effectively entered by force; it can only be entered by contemplation, with respect. The perception of Now comes to fullness in Open Space, safe space, sacred space.

Organizations operating in Open Space manifest themselves in their totality, a fancy way of saying, "It's all there, warts and all." In the concrete situation of an Open Space event, all those who care are invited to share in the communal process of being and becoming fully what they are. As strangers, close colleagues, or both, participants enter the circle, and before words are spoken, a rich field of shared meaning emerges in the void, confronting and connecting everyone. Even when antagonists occupy the same space, as in competing departments, interest groups, peoples, or professions, they are united by a common concern for the issue at hand, be that the future of a country (Canada), the design of a project (AT&T), or the creation of doors (Boeing).

The initial experience is one of intense focus and concentration. All eyes are fixed on an empty space, attention is riveted on nothing. The emptiness is mirrored by a blank wall, soon to become the bulletin board, and then site of the marketplace. But in the moment, there is nothing. Now is very concentrated, very dense; *pregnant* would be an appropriate word.

Then a virtual explosion is triggered as the participants flood the center, borne by expectation and anxiety, and bringing that which has heart and meaning for them. Prospectively, the moment of explosion takes forever to materialize. In retrospect, it happens in an instant, and suddenly there is a sense of presence—the Now grows.

The intense activity at the core spills outward, breaking through the circle, heading toward the wall. People and ideas expand, defining new space, creating new circles. In a dance as old as humankind, the circle forms and reforms, defining new centers of meaning.

As the initial organizing meeting closes, multiple circles are established in breakout rooms and corridors. Fractal patterns emerge, always the same, but never quite, following the strange attractors of passion. An organic, living being appears, creating its own time and space, a Now peculiar to itself. Always the same, but never quite, always expanding, but never disconnected.

Fantasy born on the wings of poesy? Perhaps, but in the moment, hard practicalities surface, design decisions are made in a fraction of the normally anticipated time. Technical details are handled with dispatch. The circle gives birth to other circles, the Now expands, and wholeness, connection, community make their appearance.

The Appearance of the Stranger

As the Now expands, a curious phenomenon takes place. That which previously had no place in the circle (the organization) is suddenly included, and the practical results can be amazing. I call it *the appearance of the stranger*, and almost inevitably, but never on a schedule, the stranger shows up.

Rockport Shoes, makers of superb accessories for the feet, held an Open Space to lay the groundwork for the next phase of its development. To that point, the company had done extraordinarily well, and the bottom line couldn't have looked better. But there was a recognition that success could bring failure if one were to fall into complacency. The whole corporation was closed and everybody, from the CEO to the gentleman who swept the floors in the distribution center, was invited to participate.

The chief financial officer was practically apoplectic, calling the exercise the million dollar meeting, by which he meant the million dollar loss. Despite his apprehensions, the corporate body assembled in its totality, and during the two–day period, no shoes came in, none went out, and no money was made. Almost five hundred people filled the floor of the distribution center, seated in concentric circles with a very large open space in the center.

The process began, and the magic of self-organization took over. People from all levels and functions came forward with what had heart and meaning for them, and in somewhat less than an hour almost one hundred areas for exploration had been identified.

One of these areas, a very hot one, was new products. The Rockport line was established, but the competitors were gaining. Doing business as it had always been done was a certain prescription for not doing business at all. In the very center of the vast distribution center floor, an intense, excited group assembled. Ideas and strategies flew in all directions. You could almost warm your hands with the heat of exchange.

I was not part of this group, indeed I rarely join groups when I am the facilitator, but I could not help but notice the mounting fervor. I also noticed a security guard, who was not even a Rockport employee, walking onto the floor from one side of the huge distribution center. He was drawn to the assembled body almost magnetically, circling around the group like a planet around the sun, until he eventually drew up a chair and sat down. Nobody objected; they made room for him. Suddenly he was not only part of the group but an active participant.

Inching his way in, he was eventually confronting a senior Rockport executive, the vice president for marketing if my memory serves me correctly. From that position, he posed his question, "Sir, I want to ask you one thing. Why doesn't Rockport sell shoes to security forces? I'll give you the answer. They don't look right."

Rockport makes some of the most comfortable and durable shoes in the world, but they are "casual" to say the least. Security forces lean toward a military style; casual is not part of their dress code. But if you had a great shoe, dressing it up in the military mode should not be a problem.

The vice president could have taken offense. After all, here was a total outsider telling the professionals how to do business. But he recognized that this stranger had just pointed out a half–billion–dollar market Rockport had never considered.

To make a long story short, in something like six hours, a new product was born. After all, everybody was there, obviating the need for endless memos and meetings up and down the chain of command. Even the dour CFO found occasion to smile, for he calculated that first–year sales could run in the neighborhood of twenty million dollars. Not too bad for a million dollar investment!

And How Big Is Now?

Now expands in funny ways, and rarely according to whatever plan may have been in place. That which was strange becomes familiar, and the bits and pieces dissolve into a more fundamental unity. In prospect, the expanding Now is often viewed with anxiety, for surely if the perceived boundaries are enlarged, things could get out of hand, control could be lost, strangers could appear who might contaminate the space and time of the organization.

Retrospectively, the expanding Now appears as a blessing. The natural, preexisting connections of life are made manifest. Newfound power and new opportunities connect, and with the wisdom of hindsight, that connection is seen as having always existed. It was only an arbitrary set of boundaries that limited the sense of possibility.

How far can the Now expand? The mystics of our world would answer: there is no limit. Now can expand though all of time and space. Indeed, with a fully expanded Now, there ceases to be any sense of near or far, past or future. It is all Now. In a word, time and space literally disappear, for it turns out they are only arbitrary constructs.

If the mystics are right, the limitations of time and space are self-imposed. Now does not expand, it simply is. It is our consciousness of Now that expands, and we are limited only by our willingness and ability to engage the journey.

At this juncture, you may understandably be asking what the strange ideas of mystics throughout the ages might have to do with the manufacture of shoes, as in the case of Rockport, or indeed with any of the time- or space-bound activities of our daily organizational lives. At one level the answer may well be nothing, and the odd notion of mixing mysticism with manufacturing may simply be an aberration of little utility.

On the other hand, if we find the world of our perception constrained, if we feel ourselves speeding out of a dead-end past on to a scary future with a very narrow window of opportunity, a little more Open Space might not be all that bad. After all, Now expanded some twenty million dollars' worth at Rockport as the gift of a stranger who was brought into the circle.

Expanding Our Personal Now: Bringing Our Whole Selves to the Party

Organizations with expansive Nows have more room for all sorts of people, and all sides of these same people. When the stranger finds welcome, so also does the stranger in each one of us. In a word, we can bring our whole selves to the party.

Remember the gardener's gift in Goa? There, in the middle of a room filled with senior people discussing important things, sat a copper pan of floating petals. The gift of an unknown and absent gardener created the focal point of conversation. Presuming that the conference results were important, and I think they were, the gardener's gift was critical to the emergence of those results. All he did was bring the flowers, which was all he had, and all that was needed.

Open Space welcomes the abundant diversity of humanity. The various flavors and shades of humankind add to the richness of the experience, as do the peculiar talents and interests of each one of us. Gardeners bring flowers, singers bring songs, and more often than not, what starts out as "pure business" metamorphoses into a life-renewing experience.

There is no predicting the gift or the giver, but when both arrive, the result is truly awe-inspiring. Several years ago a major communications company held an Open Space in an effort to heal a terrible wound. The ravages of reengineering and downsizing, combined with a major natural disaster, brought one region of the company to its knees. The heart was broken, the system was broken, and the Spirit was in terrible shape. Manifest alienation and hostility between labor and management were palpable, and the opening circle felt rather like a combined declaration of war and a wake. More than a few participants were quite prepared to declare defeat and go home.

But the ending was quite different. As we sat in a circle for the last time, one of our number, a union member, looked around the group and said, "As some of you know, I have had some trouble with my family, but I want you all to know that I have found my family, and it is you." Out of his pain and vulnerability, one who felt as a stranger had found family and come home. His words became a gift of affirmation for everybody present, acknowledging and confirming the community of interest that could provide for the healing required. It is a funny thing, Open Space very often feels like home.

All of this can be most unsettling for those of us who have positively determined that business and personal life shall remain forever separate. Doubtless, reasons exist for this separation, but there is a price as well. In days such as ours, requiring the ultimate in personal commitment to the highest standards of excellence and creativity, only the involvement of the whole person will be sufficient. Whether the issue is competitive advantage, social responsibility, or ecological restoration, anything less than our total best just won't do.

If the times require our total presence, many of us are also, and quite independently, coming to the conclusion that hiding some aspect of ourselves just won't work any more. If going to work means being a partial person, it is time to seek alternative employment. This is not about dropping out, as might have been the case in the 1960s. It is really about dropping in, with both feet and everything we've got.

It is positively amazing how much power can be released when the whole person, including the strange and different parts, is invited to show up. Such is the invitation of Open Space, and the results speak for themselves in terms of organizational accomplishment. The results in terms of individual accomplishment are equivalent. Surprise! The unthinkable is thought, the impossible is accomplished, and most of all—it was fun!

When people are having fun, even in the midst of the most dire circumstances, there can be little doubt that good and useful things will happen. There can also be no doubt that whole people are involved. Genuine fun admits no pretense, and as a fringe benefit, stress is nowhere to be found. When what you do and *what you want to do* are the same, stress disappears from your vocabulary.

The eleventh century Sufi poet, Rumi, captures the moment exquisitely.

> *Today, like every other day, we wake up empty*
> *and frightened. Don't open the door to the study*
> *and begin reading. Take down a musical instrument.*
>
> *Let the beauty we love be what we do.*
> *There are hundreds of ways to kneel and kiss the ground.*
>
> —translated by John Moyne and Coleman Barks
> (Threshold Books, 1984)

Such are the gifts of Open Space.

Open Space Print and Video Resources from Harrison Owen

Spirit: Transformation and Development in Organizations
An introduction to the world of Spirit and Open Space in organizations. Theory, practice, and case studies make up what Terry Deal (coauthor of *Corporate Cultures*) described as "a treasure of knowledge and lore."
(1987, $20, Abbott Publishing)

Leadership Is
Everybody says there is a crisis in leadership. Actually, there is plenty of leadership and it resides in all of us. *Leadership Is* describes, in very practical terms, the rights, duties, obligations, and opportunities of this new leadership.
(1990, $20, Abbott Publishing)

Riding the Tiger: Doing Business in a Transforming World
Modern chaos theory and ancient traditions combine in *Riding the Tiger* to describe the process of transformation in organizations.
A new organizational life form is coming into view called the Inter-Active Learning Organization, and it appears each time Open Space Technology works its magic.
(1991, $20, Abbott Publishing)

The Millennium Organization
We will shortly enter the next millennium and also move from the style of organization where authority descends from the top and control is everything, to something quite new. In the new millennium organization, we will experience high learning, high play, appropriate structure and control, genuine community, and the primacy of Spirit. At least that is the story.
(1994, $20, Abbott Publishing)

Tales From Open Space (edited by Harrison Owen)

Open Space Technology has been used by many people all around the world. In this book, journalists, practitioners, and just plain folks share their experiences and reflect upon the outcomes.
(1995, $20, Abbott Publishing)

Expanding Our Now: The Story of Open Space Technology

A new stand-alone companion for *Open Space Technology: A User's Guide*, *Expanding Our Now* is an exploration of what OST is, how it developed as a process for meeting management, and how and why it works all over the world. *Expanding Our Now* provides historical background, with case studies, and delves into the questions of why and how Open Space works.
(1997, $24.95, Berrett-Koehler Publishers, or your favorite bookstore)

Learning in Open Space (thirty-minute video)

Produced by five-time Emmy Award winner Anne Stadler, this video introduces you to the Open Space experience.
(1990, $65, Abbott Publishing)

To order Abbott Publishing materials, make checks payable to Abbott Publishing in U. S. dollars. Shipping charges are $2.50 per item in the United States. Special shipping, foreign shipping, and quantity discounts are available. Please call or email for details. Send prepaid orders to:

Abbott Publishing
7808 River Falls Drive
Potomac, MD 20854
Tel: 301–469–9269
Fax: 301–983–9314
Email: own@tmn.com
Open Space Homepage: http://www.tmn.com/openspace

The Open Space Institutes in the United States and Canada

Join the Open Space Institute

If you believe the current ways of organizing are sapping our collective energies, then join us in growing Open Space.

Creating learning communities.

Connecting people with their ability to create what they want in their lives.

Increasing creativity in the work place.

And having FUN doing it!

What is the Open Space Institute?

The Open Space Institute is a learning community that provides space for:

- Mutual Support and Connection
- Mentoring and Being Mentored
- Learning and Research

Since 1985, Open Space Technology has been free for the taking. Never a proprietary product with a franchise fee attached, Open Space is available for those who need it. But there is a responsibility: to share experiences and grow the knowledge base. Open Space is longer a strange thing, done by a few. There is a critical mass of experience involving thousands of people all over the world. Sharing and growing that experience is what this Institute is all about.

Please join us in growing the Open Space Institute.
—Harrison Owen, Winter 1997

Emerging Focus Areas

- *Education* in facilitating Open Space Technology.
- *Publishing* information related to self–organizing systems includ-ing books, videos, multi–media, and occasional papers.
- *Research* into the use and impact of Open Space: why it works, when to use it, how to sustain its effects.
- *Clearinghouse for learning* through a web site, sharing research findings, supporting conversations and networking.
- *Special Programs* to support of a variety of communities of public interest including health care, education, community development.

Want to Know More?

- Visit our web site at http://www.tmn.com/openspace
- Contact us at osi@tmn.com or in Canada at Ipasoc@inforamp.net
- Or call Peggy Holman, at (425) 643–6357 in Canada, call Joan DeNew (905) 549–7956

Why Join Us?

1. To be part of a community exploring the possibilities of self–organizing systems.
2. We provide a place to publish your work.
3. You'll receive discounts on publications.
4. Your name and information you want to share about yourself is published on the web site.
5. This is your chance to be part of launching something that in its own small way is about changing the world: where communities of learning and action are formed by committed people who bring themselves, in all their uniqueness, to play.

How to Join

Send your name, address, phone, fax and e-mail address along with a check for annual dues of $70 (or what you can afford) in US dollars and drawn on any US bank to:

> Open Space Institute
> 15347 SE 49th Place
> Bellevue, WA 98006

We have applied for 501(c)(3) status, which makes your dues tax deductible.

In Canada, the fee is CND $35 sent to:

> Open Space Institute of Canada
> c/o Larry Peterson
> 41 Appleton Avenue
> Toronto, Ontario M6E 3A4

Interested, but not yet ready to write a check?

You can stay in the loop by sending an e-mail message to **osi@tmn.com.**

Index

About the Author

Harrison Owen is president of H. H. Owen and Company. His academic background and training centered on the nature and function of myth, ritual, and culture. In the mid–1960s, he left academe to work with a variety of organizations, including small West African villages, urban community organizations (both in the United States and in Africa), the Peace Corps, regional medical programs, the U. S. National Institutes of Health, and the U. S. Veterans Administration. Along the way, he discovered that his study of myth, ritual, and culture had direct application to these social systems. In 1977, he created H. H. Owen and Company in order to explore the culture of organizations in transformation as a theorist and practicing consultant. Harrison convened the First International Symposium on Organization Transformation and is the originator of Open Space Technology. He is the author of *Spirit: Transformation and Development in Organization; Leadership Is; Riding the Tiger; Open Space Technology: A User's Guide; The Millennium Organization;* and *Tales From Open Space.*

Some of Harrison Owen's client engagements and presentations include: Owens/Corning Fiberglas, Procter and Gamble, Dupont, Eastern Virginia Medical Authority, Shell/Netherlands, Shell Tankers (Dutch), Shell/Canada, the French Ministry of Telecommunications (PTT), the U. S. Forest Service, the U. S. Internal Revenue Service, Jonathan Corporation, the U. S. Army, Ikea (Sweden), Statoil (Norway), SAS Airlines, Young Presidents Organization, City University Business School (London), Gronigen University Business School (Holland), Taj Hotel Group (India), Congresso de Desarrollo Organizacional (Mexico), PepsiCola (Venezuela), National Education Association, Toronto–Dominion Bank (Canada), American Management Systems, American Society of Training and Development, Scott Paper, TELCEL/Venezuela, the American Society of Association Executives, the Presbyterian Church (USA), the Accor Hotel Group (France), Ermetek Corp (South Africa), the Union of International Associations (Belgium), Rockport Shoes, Corporate Express, the World Bank, AT&T, IBM, USWEST, the Organization Development Network, Lucent Technologies, and the Bank of Montreal.

Berrett-Koehler Publishers

Berrett-Koehler is an independent publisher of books, periodicals, and other publications at the leading edge of new thinking and innovative practice on work, business, management, leadership, stewardship, career development, human resources, entrepreneurship, and global sustainability.

Since the company's founding in 1992, we have been committed to supporting the movement toward a more enlightened world of work by publishing books, periodicals, and other publications that help us to integrate our values with our work and work lives, and to create more humane and effective organizations.

We have chosen to focus on the areas of work, business, and organizations, because these are central elements in many people's lives today. Furthermore, the work world is going through tumultuous changes, from the decline of job security to the rise of new structures for organizing people and work. We believe that change is needed at all levels—individual, organizational, community, and global—and our publications address each of these levels.

We seek to create new lenses for understanding organizations, to legitimize topics that people care deeply about but that current business orthodoxy censors or considers secondary to bottom-line concerns, and to uncover new meaning, means, and ends for our work and work lives.

See next page for other books from Berrett-Koehler Publishers

Other leading-edge business books
from Berrett-Koehler Publishers

Open Space Technology
A User's Guide

Harrison Owen

Open Space Technology: A User's Guide *is just what the name implies: a hands-on, detailed description of facilitating Open Space Technology—a remarkably successful meeting strategy that has been used all over the world. OST enables self-organizing groups of all sizes to deal with hugely complex issues in a very short period of time. This practical, step-by-step user's guide—written by the originator of the method—details what needs to be done before, during, and after an Open Space event.*

Hardcover, 175 pages, 8/97 • ISBN 1-57675-024-8 CIP • **Item no. 50248-201 $24.95**

Discovering Common Ground
How Future Search Conferences Bring People Together to Achieve Breakthrough Innovation, Empowerment, Shared Vision, and Collaborative Action

Marvin R. Weisbord & 35 International Coauthors

This book *brings together cases from around the world of a breakthrough approach—called a "future search conference"—to strategic planning, empowerment, consensus building, and whole systems improvement. It shows how all types of business, government, and nonprofit organizations are successfully using this approach to create shared vision, innovation, commitment, and collaborative action that exceed what people thought possible.*

Paperback orig., 460 pages, 1/93 • ISBN 1-881052-08-7 CIP • **Item no. 52087-201 $28.95**

Reawakening the Spirit in Work
The Power of Dharmic Management

Jack Hawley

Hawley responds *directly to a widespread desire for spirituality at work, offering a practical vision of work permeated with "dharma"—deep integrity fusing spirit, character, human values, and decency. Through real-life examples, He shows how people can create improved workplaces and more resilient, effective, and successful organizations. He shows how leaders and managers who are motivated by a spiritual vision will liberate the best in people, and explains why all leadership is spiritual.*

Hardcover, 224 pages, 5/95 • ISBN 1-881052-22-2 CIP • **Item no. 52222-201 $24.95**

Available at your favorite bookstore, or call (800) 929-2929